Margene Wiese-Baier

How Do You See Me Inside Out ?

HE sees me as Beautiful!

Primix Publishing
485c US Highway 1 South
Suite 100
Iselin, NJ 08830
www.primixpublishing.com
Phone: 1-800-538-5788

Published by Primix Publishing: 12/10/2024

ISBN: 979-8-89194-195-3(sc)
ISBN: 979-8-89194-196-0(e)

Library of Congress Control Number: 2024911225

PRIMIX
PUBLISHING
THE WRITE CHOICE

Dedication

With every book I write, I Dedicate them to my Parents, Curtis Allen Wiese SR and Margaret Ann Wicklund-Wiese.

Through them, I was Born. Through them, I gained my gifts and talents. Through them, I was given the knowledge of knowing whom Jesus is. Through them, I felt secure in knowing that they would Protect me and Love me. As I grew, they taught me many things that I hold dear to my Heart. They taught me a Person's color did not matter and to be kind and loving to anyone and everyone, but also to use Wisdom in becoming friends with people that would not take advantage of a kind Heart. That one has been hard for me sometimes, being so Naive and too trusting.

My Dad showed me good work ethics, but sometimes I wish he could have been home with us more than being at work. Mom showed me that she knew me better than I knew myself. She encouraged me that School just wasn't as important to me as it was to my Sister. The best thing my Mom taught me was about Jesus. I think she was talking to me about HIM before I was even *born. I know now that HE knew me before the Foundation of the earth and before I was even placed in her womb.*

I loved my Parents with a Love that will last all Eternity. My Mom went to Heaven in 1985, and I still miss her, but I know I will see her again in Heaven. She is taking care of my daughter Danielle and all my pets, including my Horse, Adia Bador, which means "Return from the Moon," and many Cats and Dogs. She was my best friend and confidant. She came to me in a Dream and told me that she wanted me to get her writing Published, and in the beginning of 2019, I was able to fulfill part of that Promise. Even though I argued with her in the Dream that I did not feel qualified to get them Published, she insisted. I am Thankful that even though others didn't think I could do it, I got the first book Published: Wymans Creek, written by Margaret Wiese. I tried to do it the way she would want it done, making sure that her faith in Jesus came out Clearly. I am Thankful.

My Daddy (92) (2019) is still with me as I write this, and He has given me support in getting Mom's books done and writing my own Stories. He has been my inspiring force. May their Legacies, their encouragements, and the teachings they have given me live through Mom's writing.

I Love you, Mom and Dad. I hope you are Proud of me. And, Mom, if you are looking down from Heaven today, May this put a Smile upon your face. When you talk to Jesus, Please give

HIM a big hug and thank HIM for giving me you as a Mom. Give Danielle a hug and all my animals and let them know I look forward in seeing them again in Heaven.

    Love, Margene

*My Dad and Mom after Dad got
out of the Navy in WWII*

(Everything written in this book is written by me unless someone else's name is attached.)

Contents

Foreword

Margene and I met in 2000 at Suncoast Worship Center, a small church in Englewood, Florida. We shared an interest in art, writing, worship, mission trips, and the pursuit of God.

I have been impressed by Margene's tenacity to get a job done. She has finished, framed, and presented her artwork as gifts to friends, assembled her mother's writing into a book, *Wymans Creek*, now published, and now she has completed her own book. Margene shares her story like she is talking to her best friend. I believe there are those that need to hear and be impacted by her account of God's faithfulness in her life.

—Nanette Love Moran

Acknowledgments

First off, I would like to Thank Abba Father, Jesus, and Holy Spirit for guiding me in writing this book, bringing back to my Memory the Important things that happened in my Life, and giving me certain People in my Life who were there to teach me the Lessons I needed to learn.

To My Readers!

This book contains writing that I put in my Notes on Facebook, so some of it is repeated in other chapters in this book. I tried to organize it by time frames, but it is a mixture that blended together that made most of the notes as individual stories. Also, some writing was written especially for this book. I did include names of some people that I asked permission from. I left out some names, because I wanted to protect them. The only people that will recognize them will be the people that have been on my Journey of Life with me. I tried to give honor to the People that influenced my Life in a Positive way. I got to know many Ministries and Love many, and I continue to pray for and love them. I found that many are on their own Journey and that Abba Father had a different plan for me. Sometimes, I have felt a little sad, because I wanted to be part of their Ministry, but HE said, "That is their Path, not yours."

Finding the Path and Destiny is a Gift that Abba Father has given us. With the Holy Spirit's guidance, we will find that we have a Destiny that no one else can fulfill. My life is not over yet, so there is more to this story, but to be written on another day. I hope you enjoy this book and look forward to the pages that are missing, because they didn't seem important at this time or they just haven't been lived yet. I tried mainly to include things that would help others. Hallelujah! In Jesus's Name!

I Am Amazed by YOU!

I have to say, I am Amazed by YOU! I was thinking about my life and the Amazing things that YOU have done for me. How I almost died instantly in March of 2009 and I asked YOU if YOU were ready to take me Home, and then said, "But if YOU still have work for me to do, I am willing to stay." Some days I wished YOU would have just taken me Home, because it has been so hard to stay. YOU had to be my Husband, My Provider and Provision, because sometimes I had no clue where the money was going to come from. People would ask me where I got the money. In some cases, I could not even tell them, "From GOD."

And you know what? It is really no one's business how GOD provides the money, but it is important to give HIM the Glory for moving others to help when you are trying to serve HIM. Okay, I am not a well-known Pastor or Evangelist, or even a well-known Prophet, but I know I was hearing from HIM every step of the way. I was not able to work because of being hurt that day in March, but people would have had me work at McDonald's. I knew that I might be pleasing people but not HIM. HE has given me talents and gifts that were lying dormant that HE was just waiting for me to use.

I was using my gift of writing and photography for Facebook, and even promoting others, but I hadn't used them for me. I had to learn who I was in HIM in order to graduate in my calling and gifting. I wanted to fly like an Eagle, but at best, I felt like I was plucked and just ready for a Chicken coop. Oh My, how I wanted to fly. I remember the day I asked the question about still having work to do, but I let what others say stop me. The enemy would seem to grab me at my jugular vein and try to stop me from speaking up for myself, telling me that I needed to be more like so and so if I wanted to work with them. Hey, you know GOD made me this way for a reason. And I now know if I wanted a friend, I would really like me.

Of course, as a KING'S KID, I can say that because HE loves me. I now know everyone doesn't have to love me, and they don't even have to like me. And I am finally okay with that. As long as I know I am treating people as I would like to be treated. I am still working on my healing, and I am willing to apologize if I hurt someone. Forgiveness is a wonderful, freeing feeling. The thing is to really mean it.

Just think, If GOD can forgive me and start fresh with me daily, I think you can too. Anyway, it is something I am working on. Okay, that is one thing you will find with me—I am pretty honest. Sorry, men, I don't put up with much. When I love you, I really love you. And hey, if you say it to me, you better mean it. And you know what? Words without action are WORTHLESS.

WORDS ARE POWER. I HAVE HAD REJECTION ENOUGH TO FILL A LIFETIME, but you know what? It was for MY PROTECTION. Not just from Men but Women too.

So, if you like me, you like me. If not, I am not going to be offended any longer. Actually, I am growing through that!

Because I don't have time to play games with people. Those games are just the enemy's way to distract me for what I am supposed to do for HIM. Love is the answer, and HIS Promises HE will keep, so if we work together for HIS Glory, we will accomplish a lot more. So let's learn to fly together like the Eagles.

I LOVE YOU, Lord Jesus Christ. My Abba Father, trusting YOU is worth everything. And Holy Spirit, Thank YOU for being the Wind beneath my wings. Soaring together, we shall help Unite not only America but the World. Love all you Eagles and Eaglets. Let's Soar Higher and Higher.

Remembering and Being Thankful for Mothers and Fathers

December 19, 2009 at 8:46am

At some point last night, it was like I heard within myself that I needed to be thankful for something that happened a long time ago. I had even pondered on it during the night, but I was apparently still asleep, so I didn't write it down. And then it was gone. I was so disappointed, because it seemed God was trying to tell me something important. "Oh God, bring it back to my remembrance," I began to say over and over again. And all that I was getting is to be thankful to my Mother and Father for their part in bringing me into existence.

And now I ponder some more about the importance of who our parents are in who we become in life. My Mom was a Writer-Author and wrote poems, songs, novels, and on and on. She was also an Artist. She also was kindhearted and generous to a fault and never said an unkind word against anyone, and if she did, she always brought it back around to the positive in the good of the person. Somehow it got conveyed to me that even if someone says something derogatory about someone, that I should not judge the person talked about, because that is the perception of the speaker, and my perception might be completely different if I met that person.

Okay, back to being thankful for my Mom and Dad. My Mom brought me up to think about others before myself. Sometimes that is a good thing and sometimes not so good. But if I can get my eyes off my own problems and focus on helping someone else, I feel better about the things I am going through. My Mom was easy to talk to and kept it to herself what a person told her. I think that is why if a person tells me something one day and asks me if I remember, it has already been forgotten, and that is how I know I won't pass someone else's business to someone else. My Mom is now in Heaven, and I truly miss her, but I know I will see her again someday. Being close to Christmastime, it is harder because that was my Mom's favorite time of year.

Then there is my Dad. I always thought I was Dad's favorite. Now my brothers and sister would probably debate me on this point and possibly win. But isn't it true every little girl wants to be their Daddy's favorite? My Dad and I have a special bond that not all people have with their Dads, and that saddens me.

When I was growing up, I wanted to learn to cook. My Mom would let me try different creations on my own, and my Dad would actually eat them. Sorry, Dad, I am just glad you didn't go into the Hospital for some of the concoctions I came up with. Well, I did learn to cook. My Dad was a hard worker and provided very well for us. Sometimes I wish that he didn't have to work so hard and could have spent more time with us. But the biggest thing I remember is that he took us on Adventures to see my Grandmother and her husband, Doc, and my Uncle John and trips to see my Uncle and Aunt and my ten cousins. My Dad was not big on plans, but he was adventurous and spontaneous, and I think that is where I get it. I am not saying the important things aren't planned out, but the fun things need to just happen for me, and I think I got that from my Dad. I like it. I like it a lot.

I think I am thinking and pondering about all this because here, it is another Christmas, and this year, I am still on my own. My family is far away, and even though I want to be with them, it isn't going to happen. But I have the good Memories of Past Christmases when I was with them. My own children are grown now, with their own little families, but even though I am not with them physically, I am with them in Spirit during Christmas Holidays.

As far as Mothers go, I think of Jesus's mother, Mary, and how she said yes to being His mom. A big job, for sure. Even though I don't worship or pray to her, I am still thankful to her for saying yes and being obedient for such a big responsibility. Being a Mother is one of the hardest jobs I know of, but it holds the most rewards of Love.

Then Joseph saying yes, that was huge. Not just any man would have said yes to such a big task. God knew who He could trust with such an endeavor.

Both Mary and Joseph were the Mother and Father to our best gift this and every Christmas, which is Jesus Christ. Our own parents did their part by saying yes to bringing us into the World, though not a perfect World, but a place where each one of us has a part in making it a better place to live. We don't have as big of a job as Jesus did, but we have our part in telling and teaching others what He did for us, and them.

I think Christmas should be celebrated every day—not the part of giving gifts or even the part about Jesus just being born, but the part that He still exists today, and Christmas is just a reminder of where His life began on earth.

Just a thought.

I would love it if you would respond with some memory you have of your Mother and Father. Only good thoughts please! This is a positive time of year and a time to remember only good things.

I hope this blessed you as much as it has blessed me in writing it.

Remember, I love you with the Love of Jesus.

Hugs, Margene

Chapter 1

My Childhood Years

Picture taken when I was a year old

I was born October 29, 1951. Mom named me Margene Annette Wiese. She combined her name and someone named Gene. Later, I would tease her that she must have had a boyfriend named Gene. We would get a good laugh out of that. To this day, I don't know if that was true or not, But I love my name, and won't let people shorten it or call me Margaret of Marge, because those are my Mom's name. My mom took the time to give me a unique name and I want to honor that. As a baby, I was a little chunky and didn't have much hair, but I was a happy baby. I was born to the best parents in the World. I often think of talking with Abba Father before I was born, and HE showed me the Parents I would be born to and showing me the life I would live and asking me if I was willing to being born, and I said Yes, knowing that the enemy was going to keep trying to kill me because he did not want me to do all that Abba Father wanted me to do. It started with me being born with my umbilical cord wrapped around my neck and the many things that happened throughout my Life. But the Good things certainly outweighed the bad.

Best part is knowing that HE would be watching out for me throughout my stay on Earth and someday being able to return to HIM in Heaven.

My Beginning of Life

At the beginning is a good place to start.

What is amazing to me is how the things done in a person's life do not always begin when they were born, but in what has transpired before they came into this World.

I have come to realize that God knew us before that visit to the Hospital or wherever we were born. That travel down the birth canal and the first breath of air outside of our mother's womb. You see, we had an option if we wanted to come to live with our families. Okay, maybe I am being out there, but if you believe Jeremiah 29:11, it sounds a little bit easier to believe. Okay there is a lot of questions you might have at this point, but it is best to leave this for you to ask God about.

So my beginning on earth was in the wee hours of the morning on October 29, 1951. My Mom told me later that I should have been born a month before, but she had some ironing that she wanted to finish, so my birth was put off. Okay, you may not believe that could happen, but it explains why I was a little chubby, swollen, and all red. My hair was almost nonexistent. A little towhead blonde. Amazingly, I later was super skinny. But on with the story. I don't remember much of being a baby, but I do remember that my Mom taught me about Jesus from a very young age. And knowing that I was loved very much. I had two older brothers, and we all looked so much alike, I think of the three Amigos when I look at our pictures together. We all look very much like our Dad.

Growing up with two brothers was trying sometimes for me, because they loved to tease me. On a road trip to my Grandma and Doc's house one time, they even wet my pants with my baby doll's bottle to make me think I had an accident.

27

Not so funny then, but they got a good laugh out of it. My brothers were pretty ornery to me, but I think they loved me.

When we lived in Kelso, Washington, our neighbor boy ran over me with my tricycle and broke my leg, and my brothers carried me home. They remember what happened more than I do. My Mom told me that the Doctor put casts on both legs, so I would not remember which leg got broken. Amazing. I had pain and would hardly be able to walk years later. Not such a good Memory, but knowing my Brothers made sure I got home will be treasured in my Memory banks for all time.

The Three Amigos. My brother Curtis Jr crying here, because he wanted something that our brother Dan had. We were quite the trio. We may have looked alike, but we definitely had very distinct and different personalities.

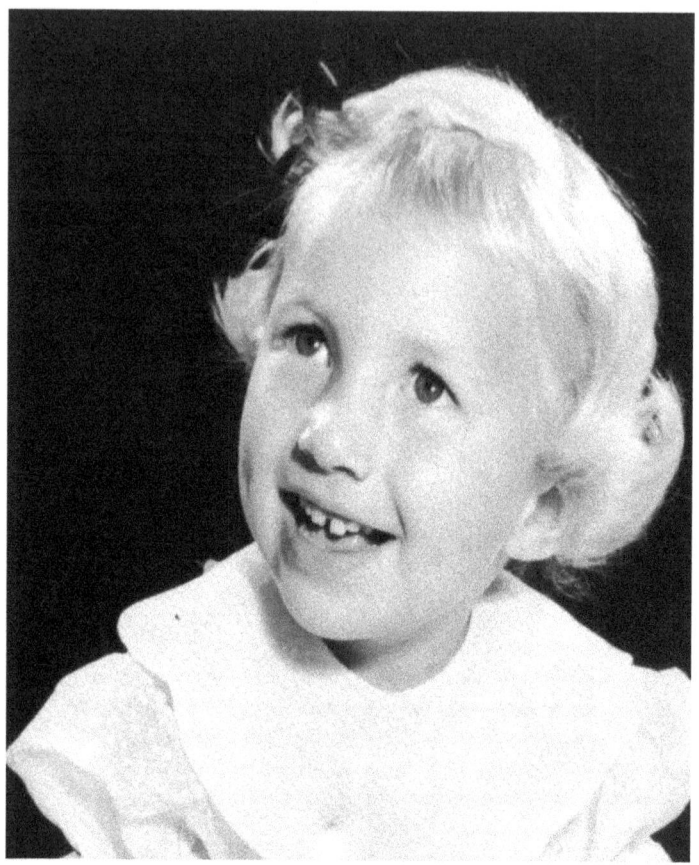

Homes

There are years that I don't really remember. I knew I was born in Longview, Washington, and lived in Kelso, Washington, by my Grandpa Wiese and a woman we called Grandma Raymond, who was not of any relation to us but treated my parents well and loved on us kids. (She did not live with my Grandpa. They were not together.)

I do remember a story my Mom told me about how she had broken off a willow switch to let the boys know if they didn't behave, she would have to use it. She would put the stick in the ground by our house, then one day she could not pull it out, because it took root. It grew to be a tree. I think it is still there to this day. They must not have needed a reminder to behave for at least the time it took for the willow switch to take root.

My Uncle and Aunt lived nearby, and we would visit them often.

We must have moved after my Grandpa went to Heaven. I am not really clear about that.

I think we first moved to Eastern Oregon. I don't remember a whole lot of what happened there like my brothers do and all their fantastic adventures, but I do remember a Teacher that the boys had who invited us to come stay at her house. She rode a big white horse to School every day. Maybe that is where I got the idea that some-day I wanted a White Stallion, and I was going to name him Snow King. I don't remember much about staying there, but I do remember her last name was Pew, or was it spelled Pugh? I remember telling my mom her name and then telling her, "But she doesn't stink." Wow, it is funny to think that as a child, I was so innocent to say that. She was a wonderful woman, and I thought a lot about her. She was tall and lanky, with silver grey hair that was threaded throughout her hair color of her younger days. She had it pulled back in a Knot-type bun at the base of her neck that was just above the collar of her blouse. She wore pants that were usually worn by women that rode horses. She was the only teacher in a one-room Schoolhouse. She has remained in my memory banks all of these years.

Wow, I almost forgot about walking home from School and how a man stopped my brother and me, and the man told my brother that I was his little girl. My brother told him, "No, she isn't. She is my sister, and you are not my Dad." We both ran all the way home. I was so thankful my brother claimed me as his sister that day (thinking how these things happened so many years ago).

We lived in other places before one of my favorite places, which follows.

I remember when we drove up to the house on 206 South C Street in Philomath, Oregon. I had the feeling of exhilaration of being Home. Seeing the big Cherry tree in the front yard right in front of the large picture window in the living room. It was full of ripe Royal Anne Cherries. Looking forward to biting into that luscious rosy red and white fruit. The owners of the house coming outside to greet us and cutting off a branch for us to take with us after we looked through the house and being toured to see the other fruit trees in the back yard. The Pear tree outside the kitchen window was later to be focused on for one of Mom's books, *The Bee Tree*. And the Quince tree in the backyard that seemed to be my Dad's favorite fruit. And then there was the Gooseberries, which made an interesting-tasting pie. A place for a Garden. And can't forget the Trellis that was covered with Roses that you could walk through to get to the front door.

I just knew it in my Heart that this was going to be our new Home. The Wiese family was going to have a New Home made just for us.

We drove away that day with the branch of Cherries, but more than that a Heart full of Anticipation that God was going to fulfill our Prayer and dream for a House of our own that we would love. Contentment and Joy was in all of our Hearts as we rode away that day knowing that we would be coming back.

Mom and Dad bought the House, and we moved in. So exciting! Mom soon got busy making the house that she had been dreaming of into a Home. Remodeling began. The Kitchen was given a fresh new color of turquoise and the living room a green like Sea Foam, with walnuts shells crushed in the paint to give it a texture that was truly unheard of before. (Walnut shells came from the trees that grew by this house.) My brothers room had beautiful wood paneling put on the walls in a natural color stain. So beautiful. My Sister and I shared a room with painted walls. Funny, I don't remember the color, but I do remember that we had brand-new bunk beds and how they were separated to become twin beds. We were naughty and jumped on my bed and broke the slats underneath. Thankfully the beds weren't ruined.

My adventures began in that little house. And I was able to go in the little woods that was in back of the house across our field. Seeking out the Lord. It was so much fun for me to just Scout out my little corner of the World. I didn't have any friends at first but was able to entertain myself. I would go outside and sing to the top of my Lungs to the Father, Son, and Holy Spirit. And sometimes wondered if they got jealous of each other, so I would try to make sure each of them got the same amount of Attention from me. I knew quite a bit about God and Jesus, but not so much at that time about the Holy Ghost. Not even knowing if HE liked to be called the Holy Ghost or the Holy Spirit. But I did know they all deserved me Loving them, and I knew they Loved me.

As the time went by, many things happened in that little house to make me love my home even more. This is where my brothers caught my little Skippy. I say "my Skippy" because she became my dog. Someone apparently abandoned her, and because she was just a puppy, she was scared and hid in a pipe under the road and driveway. One day my brothers got on both ends of the opening and caught her. I was so excited, and so were my brothers. She didn't look like any particular kind of dog, but she was black as coal and had dark brown eyes as shiny as a penny that had not seen any years of wear. My brothers asked me what I wanted to name her, and I said, "Skippy," a name that was given to some other dogs we had before. They were not surprised. I loved her with all of my Heart, and she loved me. We were pals, and we went everywhere together. She went to the woods with me and was my little protector. She would go outside and listen to me sing. I sang mainly at the end of the driveway. She slept on my bed, but I soon found out she did not like being under the covers. Even though I was cold, she soon got too hot, because of her thick coat of fur. She grew up to be a beautiful little Cocker Spaniel. She had the Sweetest Personality and loved my brothers and sister and Mom and Dad. She was loved by the other dogs in the neighborhood and soon became Mommy to many puppies. And even let other animals nurse. Dad had brought some kittens home, and she became their Mommy. I was sure they were wild kittens, but no one seems to remember what kind. Skippy was a Special dog.

Dad had a friend that brought a big Boxer over to us. We all thought he was a pretty cool dog. He let my little sister crawl all over him. He did not mess with Skippy. Soon we saw him for who he really was—a killer! My brothers raised Chickens, and this dog was killing them, and then Dad brought home a little wild kitten. That's what I remembered it being. Dad tells me it wasn't, but that is how I remember it. A baby Bobcat. I tell ya, I am sure it was. Well, I guess it does not matter, cause that Darn dog killed it. That dog scared the Garbage Man, barking at him and chasing him. It would have been funny if he would have been playing with him, but this dog was seriously mean. But not mean to us or my baby sister. Mom asked Dad to get rid of the dog because she was afraid he would turn on us and we would get hurt. Because of all that this dog was doing, Dad finally gave the dog back to his friend. The funny thing is the Garbage man told us later that he got a Boxer and it was nothing like ours. It was Gentle and Loving. Funny, ours was gentle to us but had a mean streak in him. It just shows you that we all have our own personalities, including animals.

Well, Skippy had puppies again. One of them only had three legs. He was so cute. But it was flooding outside, and I put him out on the porch to go potty, and a few minutes later I went out to get him and he was gone. I cried and cried. I felt so guilty leaving him out on the porch by himself, not thinking he would go in the water. I looked and looked after the water receded, but of course, I never saw him again. A sad lesson to learn for a child.

Life goes on, but certain things continue to haunt your mind, and I think about that little puppy from time to time. I often wondered if someone came by in a boat and picked him up. Skippy had many more batches of Puppies. I do not know why my parents didn't get her spayed, but it sure was fun having puppies around. And we never had any problems finding loving homes for them.

Mom and Dad had a friend that had a little Schnauzer. I quickly fell in love with her. Not to replace my love for Skippy, but they seemed to love each other too. An older female friend of Mom and Dad's asked us if we could take care of her while she went on vacation, and they said yes. She ended up having puppies while she was with us. We must have had her for a while, giving us time to become really attached to her. The day came when we had to give her back not knowing she would be giving her to someone else. I felt so hurt that she did not give her back to us. Again, life goes on, but that doesn't mean things don't hurt at the time.

I loved that house and never wanted to leave the house on C Street, but the time came when Dad needed to get another job, so my Parents ended up selling my beautiful home, and we moved to the Oregon Coast to a little place called Wandamere. It was kind of a strange place, because the house we moved to was a lot like the house on C Street, and we got to know the people in the little community. Some were downright out of a book. The little old man that could have been the crooked man in the poem and his Granddaughter. We became friends with a family that had several boys and one that I had such a crush on. I guess I scared him. I had thought all these years that I scared him because I was a lot older, later finding out that we were only a year apart. I became best friends with the daughter and went to movies with her and her dad. He ran the theatre in the town of Waldport, Oregon, and it was so much fun being able to go to the Movies so often. One night on the way to the theatre, we were talking about Dads and their daughters. I was telling him that Dads should not do certain things to their daughters, and he said unless the Dad thought he could teach her something. That night it made me wonder about him. I did not realize until years later that he wasn't such a good Dad after all.

I do remember one night walking home with my Mom from visiting them that he jumped out from the bushes. My Mom had a willow switch in her hand, and Mom beat him with it. He deserved it, because he scared us so bad. And maybe my Mom knew something about him that the rest of us didn't know at that time. She did not trust him.

My sisters and my room faced the woods, and so Mom had not put up Curtains yet. I was in the bedroom getting dressed and looked out the window, and the oldest boy was looking in the window. He was a peeping Tom. I was horrified. He was caught and got into trouble. I don't know if I even talked to him after that. But I wonder if his Dad was secretly telling him, "Good for you." He was a sick man, and he passed some bad stuff down to his sons.

I was still good friends with the daughter but was not as trusting around the boys and the Dad.

High School was fun, but I had a hard time in some of the classes. I felt like I was stupid half of the time and couldn't seem to comprehend what was going on, and it was frustrating trying to do homework, let alone learn anything.

My friend said that she saw me as becoming one of the Popular girls. Everyone talked to me, and I was even getting noticed by the boys. I was enjoying that part of going to School there.

The Beach was right across the highway from Wandamere, so we could go to the Beach almost anytime we wanted to. The Oregon Coast is not warm, but cold most of the time, but it was fun. My oldest brother came to visit, and one of the neighbor women and a bunch of us went to the beach and started walking out into the water hand in hand. It was a lot of fun, but probably not the safest thing to do especially at night, but it was fun at the time. I am not sure, but I think this woman was Married, but she seemed to be showing off for my brother. I am thankful that none of us drowned. Brrr! It was so cold. Sometimes a bonfire was built, and we would roast hot dogs and toast marshmallows, yummy. So much fun. Life was good. Even though we were in a Strange place, it was special time in my life.

My Dad was soon going to lose his job, and he was going Salmon fishing a lot. We sure got tired of eating Salmon, but it is a luxury now to have a good Salmon Dinner.

We were going to move back to Philomath, but my house was gone, and we weren't going to get it back. I wanted to go home, but that was just not going to happen. The people that bought it was paying an unbelievable low payment of $35 a Month. They sold the back field to the City, and they were dividing It and putting whatever they wanted on the Land. My little woods was gone. I was disappointed, but again Life goes on. For years after, I had dreams of my beautiful home, going through each room and even remember seeing Jesus walk through the Hallway by my room. My Mom told me that it was probably my brother, because he was sick. I told her, "No, it was definitely Jesus dressed in a white dress-like garment." I think HE came to heal my brother because he was not sick the next day.

We would have to find a new home. My Mom and Dad found a wonderful couple that rented us a home on Main Street, and later they bought the house. It was a nice enough house, but my heart was still loving the house on the end of the Street. The adventures were not as fun as on C Street, but I grew. I was not going to be Popular like I could have been in the High School on the Coast, but I was taught to not be a follower but to be whom God made me.

I started saying "Hi, People!" They seemed to like that. I seemed to coin the phrase. I had met a new girl, and we became great friends. She was funny, and even though she didn't know it, she was teaching me to be a fun, funny person. I was loving making people laugh. I even was the bold one when it came to talk in front of people. In Homemaking, a girl was so shy that my teacher paired us up. I had to step up to the plate, and I did it. I was in disbelief because I was always the shy one when it came to presenting something in class. I still was having trouble in some of my classes, but my Mom did not push me. She seemed to push my Sister, and I could not understand why she did not do that to me, but she saw me more as an Artist. I loved to sing too, and I am thankful now that she knew who I was back then.

My brothers soon got Married, so it was just my sister and my parents and me living in the house. At first, my sister and I had a bedroom together. I really hated that. So when my brother got Married, I took over his room in the basement. I loved it because it was like having my own Apartment. I was thankful I still had my little Skippy.

One day I was looking in Skippy's eyes and saw a white glaze over her eyes, and I started sincerely praying for her. After I opened my eyes, I looked into her sweet eyes and they were Crystal clear. She could see me. God answered my prayers in Jesus's Name. I told my Mom. She asked me to pray for her. I thought she was making fun of me, but I still prayed for her, and God answered my prayer the goiter on her neck went away. I didn't know it then, but HE had given me the gift of Healing. I know HE used my Grandma Grace to teach me how to pray. By using Animals then and later being able to pray for People.

Today I know my Mom was not making fun of me but giving me an Opportunity to use my gift by Praying for her. She truly believed more in me than I did in myself. I am finding that Parents love each Child, but the Love and belief in their gifts can be different.

Thankful!

Singing Even in Pain

One thing I really loved doing was singing. I would go outside and sing to Abba Father, Jesus and to the Holy Spirit at the top of my lungs. I remember having to have my tonsils removed and almost bleeding to death. I remember the Ether they used to put me to sleep with and how awful it smelled. I felt like I was dying. I had nightmares while I was under. When I came to, since I was bleeding so much, they put me to sleep again. I guess they had scraped a vein or something, and it caused me to almost bleed to death. From then on, my Mom was very careful with me and gave me Vitamin K to help my blood clot.

That was not the first time the enemy tried to kill me. And it wasn't the first time that I had people around praying for me and Loving me back to Life.

Like I said earlier the first time was when I was born the umbilical cord was wrapped around my neck. Then my brother's friend knocked me over while I was on my tricycle and broke my leg. The doctors put a cast on both of my legs, so I would not remember which leg was broken. Wow, that must have been something for my Mom to deal with—two rambunctious boys and a little girl in casts on both legs. Thankfully, I healed, but had leg aches from time to time afterwards. I still have them to this day.

I can't remember my Dad's Dad very much, if any, but I was always told what a great guy he was. My brothers remember him better and it makes me wish I knew him. My Mom always talked very fondly about him and told us stories of all the things he did for her, and how kind he was toward all of us. I know that Dad wanted to live with him when he was young, but was prevented from living with him, and was moved to foster homes one after another. He finally got to live with a family named Miller. I remember going and staying with them, and my brothers came too.

On Sunday I went to Church with Mr. and Mrs. Miller and everyone was crying, and I asked Mrs. Miller why they were crying, and she said, they are crying for Happy and that satisfied my young mind. I am glad my Dad got to experience at least one loving family while he was growing up, because a lot that happened to this day has left a scar on his life. He was later allowed to live with his Dad that he loved so much.

Elk Picture from Pixabay

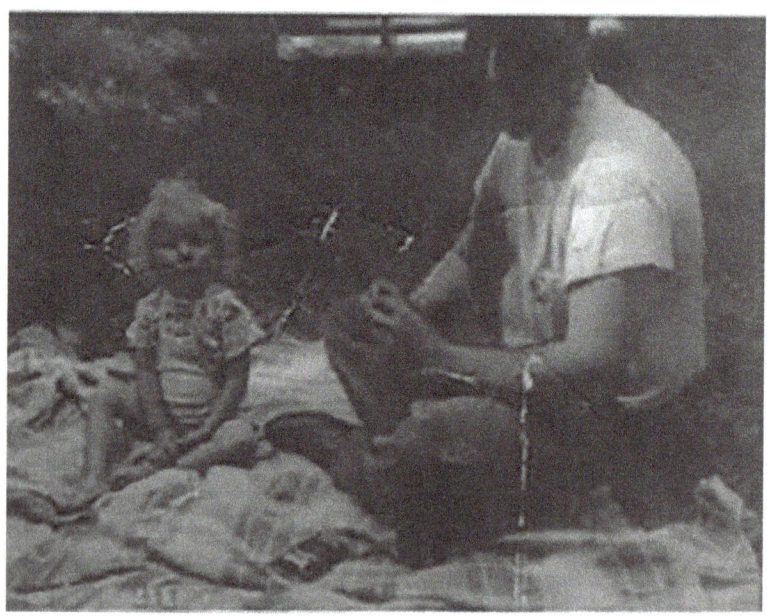

Picture of me on a Picnic with my Dad and Mom. When I look at this Picture, I remember going hiking up in the mountains with my Daddy and riding on his shoulders and seeing a beautiful Elk and shrieking with glee and Dad trying to get me to be quiet, but I just couldn't contain my excitement. The Elk looked at us and ran away. This was a good Memory. I do wish that my Dad would have captured this event on a Camera, but it being remembered by both of us is truly a Treasure that no one can take away from us. Riding on his shoulders that day made me feel loved and safe. I know there are many little girls that feel the same way. Looking back to those times is Precious.

The Christmas Disappointment!
Grade School Party!

One Christmas at School, we got to draw names of one of our classmates to buy a present for them. It was fun imagining what the person bought me. The day came when I didn't have to imagine what they bought me anymore. I was happy with the present I bought for the classmate I drew. There were giggles and laughter and "thank yous," "ews" and "aws," and then the boy that drew my name handed me my present—actually, they were presents. How excited I was when I got more than one present. They were all wrapped, not wrapped very nicely, but what could I expect from a boy? So with everyone was watching, I opened the first one. I took my time unwrapping the present, and my classmates were cheering me on. Wow, what happened next was a shock, to say the least. Not just for me, but for the other kids as well. It was a model airplane, and one of the wings was broken. I am sure a tear formed in the corner of my eyes. Then I opened the next one, hoping that it would be something I really wanted. I opened it up, and it was a box of mixed chocolates. Again, as I opened the box, I was shocked to see that someone had already enjoyed eating my chocolates. I know I tried to hold back the tears, but I am sure they flowed.

I went home, and my Mom tried to comfort me, but to no avail. She tried her best trying to explain to me why the boy did what he did, but no matter what she said, my heart was broken. Unfortunately, I could not understand how or why he would be so cruel to give me things that were once his, broken or eaten. Even the candies that were left were indented with his fingerprint.

What happened next was something that was so unexpected. The girls from my class showed up on my doorstep. My Mom asked them to come in. I do not remember how many girls showed up, but I do remember some of the girls. I did not even know that these girls liked me, and maybe it was them seeing what happened softened their heart towards me. They felt so bad for what happened and told Mom and me how sorry they were that the boy was so thoughtless. They started giving me presents to make up for what he did. I was truly amazed that this was happening.

To this day, I do not know why the boy gave me those presents. I think of those girls and am thankful that they had the compassion that day. I have not forgotten what they did. I think of all that goes on today at the schools is so harmful.

I am thankful we were allowed to pray, and God was still allowed to be talked about.

This happened while I was in Grade School. Not the only hard thing that happened to me in School, but one that affected these girls' hearts to see me as someone that needed their compassion.

I hope this shows someone out there that sometimes as humans, we need to allow our hearts to guide us. As a Christian, this is how the Holy Spirit shows us the way.

Growing Up A Lutheran

When I went to church with my Parents, I would stay in the service with them. I would lay down on the pew with my head on my Mom's lap. I felt so safe and secure in knowing that my Parents loved me. Also, feeling kind of grown up to be allowed to stay in the Sanctuary instead of going with the kids into the Sunday School Classes. I would only go when Mom taught the Class. So anyway, I would be quiet while the Pastor spoke, but sometimes I wanted so much to speak up and tell him that God would not be pleased with what He was saying. Those were the times when He was saying that the other Denominations were not going to Heaven, only the Lutherans. I know my Parents did not agree with the Pastor, Especially my Mom. My Mom was one of the most loving people in the World. She is the one that taught me about Jesus, as I said before.

In writing this now, I did not know about other Religions, only other Churches.

As I lay there, I felt Jesus letting me know that He loved many even the Catholics that the Pastor was telling us that would not go to Heaven. HE was letting me know that the Pastor would be surprised who would be in Heaven.

Church was so different then than the Churches I go to now as an Adult. But it was a good base. The Lutherans were so quiet. My Mom was faithful to her beliefs. Most of all, she Loved Jesus with all her Heart and continued to endorse that belief in me.

I do believe we talked about what the Pastor said that day. He had talked about it many other times. But I am sure others did not say to him that he shouldn't put other Churches down. The Pastor looked to me like a very stern man. I did not talk to him much. I think I was maybe a little afraid of him. Even at a young age, I knew that we need to be respectful of Adults. I do remember his wife almost seemed like Royalty. She was beautiful and dressed to the tee, and she also wore hats. My Mom wore hats then too, along with the other women. She was Stylin'! What people would call a Diva today. She just went to Heaven this year of 2020. I know many will miss her, but she is in a much better place.

To be honest, I do not remember the Sermons that the Pastor gave, but I do remember He was very Judgmental of other Churches. The Pastor is not here anymore. I do not know if Abba Father dealt with him about what he said, but I know that isn't my problem, but I do pray that He is in Heaven. I know he loved Jesus and that he was a good man.

I have learned that on this Journey we call Life, we will start differently and grow to know Jesus the way HE wants us to. Our Destiny! I am also glad to know that I will see all of them again in Heaven. For a longer time.

Trip to Minnesota from Oregon in the Old Bread Truck

I am not sure how old my brothers and I were when we took the long trip from Oregon to Minnesota, but I remember it was a very long trip. My Uncle borrowed the Bread Truck he drove for his work. And I remember that we all can be thankful that we all made it back to tell about it. The reason I say that is, because as you know, kids have a habit of complaining on a trip. It wasn't just my brothers and myself on the trip with my Uncle but also my Aunt and my Mom and all my Cousins. All together, there were seven girls and three boys. I don't think all of them were on this trip because some weren't even born yet.

All of us kids were bunched up in the back of the truck, being tossed about yet feeling scrunched up like sardines. Okay, yes there was a lot of complaining and for good reason. We went around a lot of sharp corners in the Mountains, sliding back and forth into each other. And you see, the exhaust system must have had a leak, and we were all getting asphyxiated! My Uncle didn't believe us—until he decided to take a nap and he learned that we were not lying. So he stopped and let us out to get some fresh air. Now can you imagine letting all those kids out on the side of a Mountain and looking down in a deep canyon. Wow, I can remember my one boy cousin almost falling off the cliff and all of us walking around like we were drunk. I do not know how my cousins or my brothers remember this, but that is what I remember.

I don't remember much about being in Minnesota, so I must have been pretty young. But I do remember eating hamburgers at my Uncle Bud's house and him making the comment that they tasted like Steak burgers. They were yummy, and I would love to have one today. And making cookies and candy with my Aunt Lynn. She worked at a home that housed men that needed help. My mom's sisters and brothers were very loving and kind. And it was fun seeing where my Mom grew up. But the most memorable thing was riding in that Bread truck, and it sure left an imprint on my mind. I sure hope they got that exhaust system fixed. And yes, I am thankful that we were able to make the trip to Minnesota.

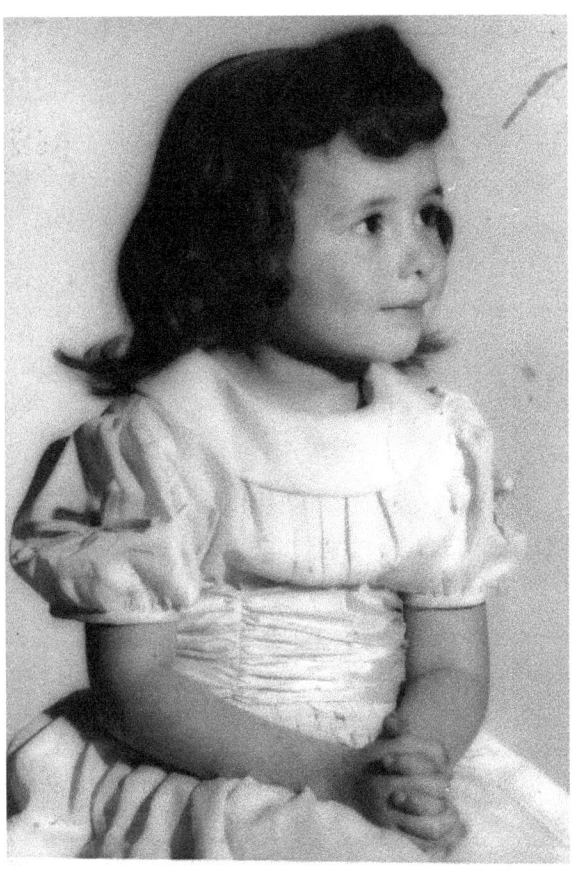

My Sister, Tami.

My brothers had each other. They were best friends, and then there I was, their little sister, but even though I loved hanging out with them, watching Westerns, I am sure I was more of an annoyance—a nuisance, really—instead of a person they wanted to have around.

So there I was, longing for a friend a sister, someone I could play with, to talk to. Believing that if I asked and prayed for a little sister that God would give me one, I Prayed as much as I could, and in Jesus's Name, I believed that she would come. My Mom wanted to help me get a little sister, and not having the faith I had to get my prayers answered, she was going to put her plan into motion. Her and Dad were going to check into adopting a little girl, but God had a different plan.

That morning, when Mom was going to call to make an Appointment at the Farm Home in Corvallis, Oregon, to check about Adoption, she was not feeling too well, so she made an Appointment with the Doctor instead. Should she have been surprised that my little sister was going to come in nine months? Yup! About nine months, I had my Prayers answered. A Sister with silky dark hair and coal black eyes. She looked like my Mommy. I adored my Sister and was so happy that she was finally here. I was now seven and would still have to wait to play with her, but I got to help Mom care for her. I was thankful that God heard and answered my Prayers.

Moving to Wandamere, Oregon—Coast Living!

My Dad had put in for a new job on the Oregon Coast, and he got it. I loved the house we lived in at Philomath, and part of me was sad that we would be moving, but part of me was excited. We were going to live in a little hole in the wall called Wandamere. It was a strange little place but enchanting. It was across the highway from the beach. Wow, it was so beautiful. The Oregon Coast is cold, but the Rocks and the water were so worth it. So we had a new beginning. The house we moved into was wonderful. It was not really big, and my sister and I had to share a room. The house backed up to a lot of trees. There were thimble berries and other kind of berries grew there. Down the road was a family with several boys and a daughter that I became good friends with. We went to School together in Newport, and she told me that I was going to be popular there. There were cute boys there that seemed to like me. She liked this one boy that lived in a house on a hill. It was a Magical place. There were beautiful Lighthouses. Wandamere was like a place directly out of a Book. There was a Grandpa that reminded me of the poem about the Crooked Man, and his granddaughter that didn't like you saying "grease." There was an older girl that wanted to throw me a Surprise Birthday party and my other friend

53

told me about it. I was pretty upset with her for telling me about it. But it was a fun party.

We did not live there much longer and moved back to Philomath. Unfortunately, Mom and Dad sold the house we had lived in. I was so sad that we no longer had the house, but they ended up buying another house. That house was a bigger house than the one we live in on C Street. We made new memories there.

Chapter 2

My High School Years

Moving back to Philomath, Oregon
My High School Years!

Hi, people! For some reason, I started saying this when I would come up to the other kids in School. I may not have been one of the Popular kids, but I was determined to be remembered as a nice girl. I had my crushes on some of the boys. The one thing that was humiliating was walking down the halls and having the boys stand along the wall watching all of us girls walk by and knowing they were talking about us. I do remember sometimes my legs felt like they were going to give out on me. I thought for sure it was from breaking my leg when I was a little girl.

There were Dances that we had, and some are more memorable than others.

Before this dance, one of my mom's friends who was a hairstylist decided to fix my hair. She knew I was a shy girl and needed a little help. She fixed my hair, and I looked so cute, so at the Dance, I was asked to dance by one of my Classmates. I was thinking about someone that I had a crush on while dancing, but thought this boy was sweet for asking me to dance, and we were doing a slow dance. The next day, I told my Mom's friend I had a good time and appreciated her fixing my hair.

At another dance, I decided to wear one of my Mom's wigs and pretend I was my cousin. See, I had long blonde hair and the wig was short, and it was brown hair. I was swinging, and it was fun to pretend I was someone else. I was very shy and quiet, but wearing a wig, I could pretend to be flirty and talkative as someone else. The problem was that no one bought it. They did not even pretend and play along. Just thinking how my hair was an important part of my life even then.

I can't say that High School were the best years of my life. I struggled with comprehending my schoolwork. I do remember one of my English teachers loved my poem about Love and asked if he could have it. I gave it to him. I have no idea what he did with it. Then another English teacher made me take a test over. I asked her why she wanted me to take it over and not the other girls. She said that I had more going for me. I really appreciated that she thought that much of me. I never felt very good about myself, but she made me feel better about things that day.

There was a History teacher that led a discussion about how people in our little town used to make black people leave. We all agreed that was wrong.

So I got through those years and wouldn't want to repeat them. Some people talk about High School as the best years of their lives. I certainly wasn't one of them. I think I was depressed, but I did not even know what depression was.

My First Real Boyfriend

In the small town I grew up in, there wasn't much to do. It seemed every time a Movie house came into town, the Churches got rid of them. So strange because it gave us kids something to do on Saturdays—Free Movies. One thing we did have was a Roller Rink that was just up the Street from where I lived. We would go on the weekends. It was always packed. And then came the boys from the Job Corp. Good-looking boys. Finally, I had a boyfriend. I was beginning to think I would never have a boyfriend. And I had one of the best-looking boys in the whole group. One of my older girl friends said to me, "I didn't think you had it in you, Margene." Wow, what did she mean by that? I already lacked confidence. But he must have thought I was pretty. At that time, I had a bump on my nose and had an ugly front tooth. My nose had gotten broken when I was younger. And I had my front tooth knocked out during a Volleyball game, playing with the boys at School. I was knocked down because the boy behind me went for the ball at the same time I did. I guess he did not think I would go for it. I was knocked to

57

the floor, and I hit the floor hard and everything went black, but the first thing I thought when I woke up was that the tooth that was out of place was knocked out, not one of my front teeth, because I liked my front teeth. They were straight, and they were pretty. I was the center of attention. It was not a flattering thing being in the center of attention with a tooth that was broken out of my mouth and blood all over. I don't know how long I was out. With everyone standing around me, and the teacher trying to bring me too. I don't think they called for an ambulance, but I remember my Mom being there. I must have been a frightful sight. I hurt and just wanted to disappear. I never thought I would feel that way, because I already felt invisible. I do remember wishing that it was my eye tooth that was knocked out, because it was not in the correct place, but no, it had to be one of my perfect front teeth. Soon to be replaced by a stark white temporary tooth that everyone would notice and think my other teeth were pure yellow. I was sick at the thought that I may never want to smile again. One girl at School asked me if I ever brushed my teeth because my other teeth looked yellow in comparison. Now that was really a cruel thing to say. I felt humiliated! So life goes on. I later went to another Dentist thinking I would get a tooth that would be an improvement, but no, another disappointment. I decided I was still going to Smile and was soon given the nickname Smiley. I did not consider myself one of the Popular kids, but it was nice being known for having a Smile for everyone.

I was thankful to now have a boyfriend. Not knowing that another girl was waiting in the wings for us to break up. Meantime, he had given me a hand-pounded metal cross that he later asked for back, so he could give it to his new girl-friend. He really liked my little sister and gave her a necklace for her Birthday. I know I was jealous of her at that point. Not understanding that he probably just saw her as a little sister, because he had none of his family near. I remember my Mom saying to my Dad, "We won't have to worry about Margene doing anything with this boy." I was a good girl, and even at that point did not want to disappoint my Mom and Dad or God either. I still think of him to this day, it would be fun to find him to see where his life led him. I do pray He found Jesus. I hope I did talk to him about our Savior.

Be a Leader, Not a Follower

I was not considered to be in the Popular crowd, but I did consider the Popular kids to be some of the nicest kids in School. I did not consider myself as one of the Smart kids or belonging to any group. I remember two Senior girls talk about how we should all be individuals: Be a LEADER, not a follower. I remember that to this day. They made a positive impact on my life that day. I did not want to follow anyone that would lead me the wrong way. I did not Drink, Smoke, or take Drugs. I was independent of people that did those things. My Mom and Dad had showed me early to always try to do the right thing. I will continue to remember this Advice that these girls gave me and treasure their Wisdom at such a young age. I do hope that more people heard their message that day, being Leaders instead of Followers. This became my Foundation for my Journey in Life.

After I Graduated from Philomath High School, we went to Portland, Oregon, for Senior day. We had dinner at a Chinese Buffet. I had never been to a Chinese buffet, so it was quite a treat for me. It was fun. So funny, kids that grew up together almost from the first grade celebrating finally making it through to the end of High School together. We then went and bowled and played pool. I was pretty good especially at Pool. The guys were so surprised. I never went out with any of them while going to School, even though I had crushes on a few of them. I don't know if any of them had crushes on me. I even had a date for Senior Prom. I kind of felt guilty because the guy should have taken another girl. I didn't realize how shy I was because I could flirt with boys at School, but didn't have anything to say to this guy. Very sad. Yup! He should have taken the other girl. She was there, though, and I think they got to dance together.

Back to the Senior outing. We had a dance that night too. A few of the guys brought booze and tried to get others to drink. But being the good little girl I was, I didn't drink. I don't know how they got by with it. It still surprises me that kids that hardly had anything to do with me talked to me and we had a good time. So now what? Life goes forward from there. Next!

Chapter 3

After-School Years

Idaho, Here We Come

Close friends to my family were going to Idaho to visit their relatives. Their Mom asked me to come with them. My Mom did not want me to go, but the friend assured her that I would be safe and that they would bring me back, so we all piled up in the Station wagon. The Dad and the Mom and their five kids. Four boys and a girl. We were going on an Adventure. I was so excited. I really liked the oldest boy and did try to get his attention, but I guess he just wasn't interested. Well, I was going to soon find out there were going to be more boys in Idaho. It was a long ride to Idaho, but we finally got there, and I got to meet all their relatives. I met their Aunt that talked me into not wearing Makeup for a while. That didn't last long. I met their cousins and found some of them truly handsome. One of their boy cousins had such a great personality. He was so funny. Nothing developed, but it was fun getting to know all of them. We had fun together. Then it was time to return home way too soon. But I came home to bad news. My beloved little dog, Skippy, had died.

I was heartbroken. I had her since my brothers caught her in the Culvert under the road. She was the sweetest little Cocker Spaniel. She had lots of Puppies, fed kitties that lost their Mom. She was a special dog. She was my best friend. More loyal than any human.

I later went and stayed with them in Salem, Oregon, before they actually moved to Idaho.

Salem, Oregon—Living on My Own!

Later I decided to get an Apartment in Salem with my Cousin that was just a year older than me. I was surprised at myself because I thought I wanted to live with my Parents forever. But my new Adventure was about to begin. I was still close enough to my home that I could go there as often as I wanted to. My cousin found a job at a Fred Meyer, and I soon nicknamed it Freddie's. We found an Apartment within walking Distance, and I found a job in a little town of Keizer, a type of Drugstore that had a Denny's Shoe Department. I loved my boss, and she loved me. She bought me a purple pants outfit, because that was my favorite color. She introduced me to her son that was in the Army. He was half Japanese and half Filipino! He was very handsome, but for some reason, I had a hard time talking to him. He wore cologne that, apparently, I was allergic to. I still went out with him probably more because of her than him. We did have a fun night together and danced most of the night at his home. His parents must have been gone for the night. I was a good girl and was still a virgin. Thankfully, he respected me, and he never forced himself on me. I am sure that was because he knew his Mom would have been upset with him, or was it that he was just a nice guy. I had met him during the Vietnam War, and he had come home. Needless to say, we only became friends. His Mom and I stayed close, though.

During the time I worked at the Shoe Store, they had a big sale, and I guess I had a little sale of my own. I was only supposed to sell the sandals in the bin, but I was selling all of them, including the ones on the racks, for the sale price. I could have gotten fired for that. The Sales Rep came in to see me. He asked me what was going on, and I told him. Thankfully, I hadn't been selling them very long before he caught it and corrected it. He gently told me what I had done wrong and told me because it was just a mistake, that I would not lose my job. What compassion! He later lost his job for something he did, but thankfully it was not because I screwed up.

One day a woman came in and gave me a certain amount of money, and I gave her more money back in change than what she had given me. And I realized it and asked her to show me the money I gave her, and she was going to refuse showing me. I was persistent, and she finally showed me, so I recounted it. I could not believe that she was going to keep the money. I was so naive thinking people were always going to be honest. NOT!

I loved working at that little Store. They were all so nice, and when we were slow in the Shoe Department, I got to help them with inventory. Since I was not their employee, they did not pay me, but I got hot cashews and different products. I think they got the better deal!

One day this guy came in and was flirting with me. I was so shy then. I never went out with him but told my boss, and she asked me why I did not go out with him. You know, I really don't know.

While living in Salem, we lived by some people that had a party one night, and I was introduced to this very handsome man. He was dis-

charged from the service for some reason and was sent back home. He asked me to go to a Drive-In movie. I was so nervous I made myself sick and could not eat, but he talked me into eating, and then we went to the Drive-In. I was not used to men that had roaming hands. He told me that I was a tease. I really liked him, but I was not going to let him touch me in areas that I knew would lead into things that I did not want to do. He did not ask me out again. I really liked him, though, and had a hard time understanding why he did not want to go out with me again. The neighbor woman tried to explain to me, but it wasn't sinking in. I later found out that he was going out with an older woman that was probably giving him everything he wanted, including money. C'est la vie!

A man moved in next door to us. He was good looking enough and had several lady friends. I thought maybe he could teach me a few things. Thankfully, he did not take advantage of my Naivety. There was a woman that every time a man came over, I would hear water running in the bathtub. I asked him why, and he explained it to me. Come on now, I was only eighteen. I'd never been away from home except to safe places. He taught me what I needed to know, and I kept my Virginity.

My cousin and I didn't have a lot of money but loved to go to the Pizza place and the bowling alley café. There was this good-looking man that worked at the pizza place, and we flirted with each other. He asked me out, but I didn't really think he was coming, and I went home to visit with my Mom and Dad. When I got back to Salem, my cousin told me that he came to pick me up and brought a dozen roses. I felt so foolish. My cousin and I went to the Pizza place and found out that he had quit and moved to Portland, Oregon. I really liked him but screwed up by going home instead of believing that he was really wanting to go out with me. My cousin and I ran into the two other men that worked at the Pizza place later, and they told me that the man I really liked had gotten Electrocuted working for the Power company in Portland. I often thought that he could have been the one that I was supposed to Marry. He was always so sweet to me when we went in there to just hang out. The other guys too, and they would make us a Pizza and tell us that someone ordered and then didn't pick it up, so if we did not take it, it would be thrown away.

The neighbor woman was in a very bad car accident, and we all knew that she could have died. She had the smell of death on her. I don't know if anyone else could smell it, but I could. She was white, and her husband was Asian. You could tell they loved each other a lot. I prayed and prayed for her, and she was getting better. I saw their friend again, but he was not going to come back to me. To him I was just a kid that was a tease.

My cousin had met someone, and the guy showed up at our Apartment. I wanted my cousin to have a boyfriend, but she was really not interested. Even though she told me that, I tried to play matchmaker. She was so mad at me for that.

Then we had a couple that moved in next to us. He liked my cousin, but he had no business liking her, because he was married. She was a very nice woman. He had a sister that later moved in with them, and she had been in the Service and was now home. Her husband wanted to get back together with her. I guess they had been in the Service together. I had found a little dog and ended up giving the dog to him, because we were not allowed to have pets. He was a very sweet little dog. I think it was the kind of dog that did not bark. I found out later it was her husband I gave the dog to. Another time that I wish I would have made a different decision.

My cousin decided that she was going to move back home. We had met a girl through some friends that I grew up with. I moved in with them for a while. I worked at the canneries with her. I stayed with them a short time then moved back home. While I lived with them, we went to Church, and she led me to believe that the Pastor was single. It turned out he had a beautiful pregnant wife with other children. Later, his Mother-in-law talked him out of being a Pastor. I still think that was wrong of her. Yes, he was very handsome, but he was totally devoted to his wife.

I Moved Back Home/Grown-Up Years

I went Home to live with my Parents Again!

Back home with my parents. I decided to buy a car. I had just got a job at Oregon State University as a Custodian, so needed transportation. It is funny the bank was right across the Street where we lived. The President of the bank helped me with the loan. I had my Dad with me to cosign, but he told me that I didn't need my Dad to cosign for me. The President of Bank offered me a job, but foolishly I told him no, because I just started the job at OSU. I was loyal. Even to this day, I wonder where my life would have led if I would have accepted his offer. Yes, I could have ended up being the President of the Bank. I guess that was not part of my Destiny. I didn't take the job but got me a Shiny little red sporty Subaru.

I liked my Supervisors and even had a crush on my main Supervisor. They would come over and have lunch with me. I would make Onion soup. They hired a man to work in the Coliseum building with me as the main Custodian. He was close to my age. I really liked him too, but he already had a girlfriend. He was trying to stay true to her. He gave me a kiss one time but told me that it couldn't happen again. He was really kind of mean and wrapped Scotch Tape in my hair. What a mess to get out. And we went to look in the Museum. That was a creepy place with all the stuffed real animals. They actually threw many of them away that were getting really old. But one day we were looking at the rocks in this little place that had lights that made my one front tooth look black. Because later after my Mom had her teeth done at a different Dentist, I decided to have my front tooth replaced. He did a root canal, and my tooth died and turned black. I did not realize that until years later when I finally had them redone to look better. The first one my Mom's Dentist put in looked good, but it left a gap in between my gums and the tooth, so he replaced it with one that was too long. Another hurt in my life. Dentists are supposed to make a person look better, not make them look worse. I lived with that tooth for many years.

Duplex Living

I moved into a Duplex with my best friend. We both worked as Custodians at OSU. I had a car, so I drove us to work and back home. It was graveyard shift, and sometimes I was so tired I know the Angels had to drive us home, because I would fall asleep at the wheel. Not very safe, that is for sure, but we would make it home. Sometimes we would stop and get freshly made donuts, warm and with just the right amount of frosting. I can almost taste how yummy they were right now as I am writing this.

We would go to dance every Friday and sometimes Saturday nights We would dance the night away. One night I saw this very handsome Italian man, and I wanted to dance with him. I was very shy, so my roommate's sister went over to him and asked him to dance with me. So I talked to him for a while and found out he was leaving for an Archeological dig in a few days. I guess I thought nothing was going to develop, so I went back and sat with my friends.

Another time this man jumped over a table to dance with me. That was quite impressive. Him and his friend asked us to go to dinner with them after the place closed. I only had one drink, a Tequila Sunrise, and I was throwing it up. I was so embarrassed. But he did not seem bothered by it. I could never be a drinker because they made me so sick. We had a good time eating together. My roommate and I went to Fred Meyer later and ran in to him and his friend. I always wore makeup, but that day I didn't, but I went and talked to them anyway. He said something about how I was brave enough to talk to them without makeup on. Even though I felt embarrassed, I thought it was more important to talk to them than ignore them and be rude. I really liked him. Later, both him and his friend moved to the same Duplexes. One night we were out dancing, and his friend's brother asked me to dance, but he was so rude and left me standing out on the dance floor. I guess he thought I had done something wrong towards his brother.

My roommate and I continued going out to dance, and one night a band came through and they wanted to come to our place. The lead singer was very handsome, but I found out that he just wanted another woman to add another notch to his belt. I made us something to eat, and for my roommate and the guy that came for her. After we ate, he made his move. Yup, he was a good kisser, but when his hands started roaming, I felt I was in trouble. Again, even though I was very attracted to this man, I was able to say no. That was the last I saw of him. Well, at least at my place.

I met many men going out dancing, but I did not take them home with me or have one-night stands. Even then I felt that would dishonor my God, my Jesus and Holy Spirit. And I certainly did not want to do that. Waiting to sleep with the One God had for me was utmost in my mind. My Parents taught me right, or was it that I knew that HE was always watching me. My friend and I Moved in a house across the Road from my brother and his wife.

My Horse, Adia Bador

My dad helped me buy a Horse. Even though I paid for it, he helped me pick her out. We had looked at Pintos and a Mare and her baby (foal) that the woman was going to give away to a good home. A little more than I had in mind. I wanted a horse that I could ride. So here we were looking at this beautiful horse named Adia Bador, which means "Return to the Moon." She was so Gorgeous, with a star on her forehead. She had the softest hair a brown that was shiny and almost the color of a shiny new copper penny. She wasn't trained yet, so I would have to find a trainer. But she stole my heart, so I bought her. I was so excited. I was twenty-one and had waited my whole life to have my dream come true of owning my own horse. I found a trainer, and she had to go there to get trained. Adia was easy to train. Even though they said the daughter thought she was going to give them trouble. I hate to say this, but they taught me some wrong things. Like kneeing her in the gut to release air. My friend and I lived across from my brother for a while and then moved to a place off of Highway 34. I was glad to move, because I was being watched and my Mom was told every time we had company. I am glad I didn't do anything I would have to be embarrassed about. But it was fun having my horse and my sister's horse right there. I could ride her whenever I wanted to. When we moved, I put Adia at a place just down the highway from the duplex I lived in. It was convenient. I later learned from a girl that had her horse boarded there. She said, "Just walk her around till the air released and then tighten up the cinch." I loved Adia. She was so special. One day I decided to ride her in the coral right outside the barn, and we were cornered by some young colts. Both Adia and I was so scared. I started praying and calling for help. No one heard me. Finally, there was an opening, and we got out of there. I went and told the owners what happened.

One day I went to see my Girl and was told that she had been run over. What? That could not be. The weird thing was that I could have put a $100,000 insurance policy on her, and I didn't because I didn't think anything could happen to her. The owner told me that the horses got out of a place in the fencing that was not repaired yet. The horses were running across the highway, and Adia looked back at her friend horse and got hit by a big truck. She was not the only horse hit, but she was the only one shot and killed. So I asked why she was shot and not the other horses. I was told that both of her front legs were broken. It was deer hunting season, and the man who shot her thought it was merciful and humane to shoot her and not let her suffer. Remembering this is painful. I went home and my fiancé tried to comfort me. I later talked to the Owner of the Boarding place, and he offered to buy me another horse or pay me what I paid for Adia. Wow, I couldn't think of having another horse then, so I took the money. That was not the best decision, because I paid out a lot of money after I bought her. That was really taking advantage of a girl that just lost her horse that she loved.

Well, Adia Bador is in Heaven with my Mom and all my other pets.

Leading Up to Marriage

While I was still living in Salem, Oregon, my Sister-in-Law's brother came to visit me. I had seen him many times while going to High School, but he had a cute little girlfriend. I was told they did everything together—hunting, Fishing, and anything he wanted to do. So even though I was very attracted to him, I kept my distance. I had this thing ingrained in me that if the man was interested in someone else, that I needed to just leave them alone. His parents had him go into the Service because they did not want him to marry this girl. I found out later that they told him that if they still loved each other after he got out, they could get Married, but that never happened. I still think they should have gotten back together, but then I would never have gotten together with him. Maybe that would have been a good thing?

I later found out that he went AWOL to come see me. Crazy, huh! But it did make me feel special.

Even though I had my own car, I started riding with a few ladies that worked as Custodians too. We rode together to save on gas money and paid so much a week.

I didn't know it then, but I was riding to work with my future Mother-in-Law. It is funny how you can have such a great relationship with someone, then you Marry their son or daughter and everything turns to a totally different Scenario. Not that I did not love her anymore, but she didn't view me the same way. Her son came to work at OSU also. He had returned home from the War in Vietnam, and we started dating. I did not realize all the damage the Service had done to him. All we did was fight. I guess I thought he would change being with me, but it just got worse. He drank a lot, and I had given him the ultimatum—Me or the Booze. Being the Naïve person that I was, I thought he chose me. I found out that was just a ruse. He was a Closet Alcoholic. We went on a trip to Idaho to dig for Opals, and every Opal I found he would crush. I know that some of them were very valuable. Was he jealous? Of me? It just couldn't be. We came back, and I did not really hear from him for several days, but I was still interested. I should have run when I had the chance. So I guess I was the one that was pursuing him. He gave me a Promise Ring, and I took it as an Engagement ring. The fighting did not stop. Was I crazy becoming more involved with him? He was so Handsome, and sometimes he would fall asleep on my couch, and I would look at him and he looked like an Angel. But when he woke up, he would change. I really cannot say I was falling deeper in Love with him, because I was becoming more afraid of him than being happy we were together.

I guess I was waiting for my Mom or Dad to tell me that I should not Marry this Man. But they liked him and never said a word. I did not realize that part of him starting fights with me was him drinking hard booze, because I just saw him drinking beer. I did not sign up for this.

My Friend Goes to Heaven

My boss's son called me and told me that she had passed away. She was my boss at Denny's Shoes in Keizer, Oregon. For some reason, I thought he was joking. What a horrible joke. She was so kind and loving to me. I can remember that she bought me a pants outfit in my favorite color, dark purple, and a light purple top. It really looked good on me.

I think I was one of her favorite people in this World. I know she would have loved it if I would have married her son, but I could not marry someone that I could not even talk to.

I had called her when I got engaged, and she was shocked, because I told her that all we did was fight. Not a good reason to get Married.

So he told me that he was not joking about his Mom. And that she really loved me. She was the one that was healthy, I thought. She was taking care of her husband. Soon after she passed, he died. I was so sad.

From time to time, I still remember how loving she was to me. She treated me like her daughter.

I know I will see her again someday. I hope I will see him in Heaven too!

Chapter 4

Marriage Years

Unbelievable, the day before getting married, I was sitting at the kitchen table with my husband to be and his sister, and he was telling me how maybe we should not get married, because our children would be teased because they would be part Japanese.

I felt crushed. How could he talk to me this way? I started crying. I knew our children would be beautiful. This man looked beautiful. Yes, I know men are usually not called beautiful, but I remember looking at him thinking he was beautiful while sleeping, looking like an angel, and then when he woke up, he was a totally different man. So here we were. Was God giving me a chance to get out of Marrying this man? I was having second thoughts after what he said to me. I went home and just thought, *If it happens, it was meant to be.* Wow, now I know that is not the way to look at things. To Not make a Decision is making a wrong decision. I have thought so much about this over the years.

So here we were at the Lutheran Church in Corvallis, Oregon. We met the Pastor, and my husband and him drank together. What? I could hardly believe it. Here he had to drink to have the courage to Marry me. What did I have? I am glad that I had my faith to help me through. So I had asked my husband-to-be to choose, me or drinking. Amazing, I thought, he picked me. How naive I was. An Alcoholic never picks you. The thing was I hadn't ever been around an Alcoholic before. Later finding out why I thought he chose me was because he was a Closet drinker and was Filling up a beer bottle with hard booze.

There we were, and as I walked toward my new husband with my Dad, I was having second thoughts. Did I love him? Moreover, did he love me? What was I doing? Was I making a Mistake? Why did he say those things to me the day before? And then he said the most absurd thing, that he saw the devil in the corner of the Church cursing our marriage from the start! What was I doing? Marriage is for a long time.

We were now Married and starting our life together. Realizing now that how a man acts before you get married is not going to change after you get Married. We had fought almost every day before we got married, and it actually got worse after we got married. What did I get myself into? I wanted Love, but it seemed that was not what I was getting. I think we both were trying, but his drinking did not help because he was a mean drunk. But the time went by so quickly. It was not all bad, but it certainly wasn't all good. I was lonelier being Married than I was when I was single. I wanted to be IN LOVE. Finding that was different than loving a person like a friend. Come on, we could not even have real conversations, and that is a very important part of a relationship.

We had that real talk after a man at his job was advised to go get treatment. He asked me what made an Alcoholic, and I told him someone that depended on drinking to solve his problems. Wow, unbelievable. The next thing I know is that he enrolled in a treatment center, and it was the beginning of a horror for me. I went with him but discovered that he was more upset about hurting other women and didn't feel bad at all about how he treated me. We were supposed to write letters to people we needed to apologize to, and he could not write one to me. I wrote one to him. And then a man asked for those that Did not have an Affair to stand up, and he did not stand. I asked him what that meant, and then other men asked him the same thing. He just laughed. I still don't know what it meant. His Doctor put him on some medication, and we actually started to get along. The others told him that he did not need it. I beg to differ—he definitely needed it. There were times I thought I could actually fall in love with him. But that was not going to happen. Sad to say. I know that he needed love just as badly as I did, but we didn't seem to know how to love each other. So our lives were spiraling out of control. We loved our children, and they were the glue that held us together.

My Business, Sugar N Spice, and My Job at the Clinic!

Since I did not have a job while the girls were little and at home, I decided to create my own business to help with the bills. I was pretty creative and sewed different things: Toaster Covers,

Clown dolls, and made Mop dolls and Sheep, etc. I would take them to different businesses to see if they would either buy them or trade for the bill. I paid many of our bills that way, mainly the ones my husband incurred. One day I went to School to talk to one of my daughter's teachers and brought one of Clowns with me, and she asked me if I could make her a Spice-colored Clown, and the name of my Business was born: Sugar N Spice. I quickly got started on making her a Spice-colored Clown. He turned out so beautiful. I started making the Spice-colored ones for other Clients. I made them to order and to what their preference was. I made some sports Clowns with Basketballs and footballs and even made a Baseball one with a little bat. I sewed the balls to look like the Sport. Everyone was extremely happy. It was very gratifying to know that they appreciated what I created for them. To this day, I still don't know if my husband appreciated me paying off his bills or not. I even went into the Car Dealership where I bought my car and sold her a doll that she had me make for her Mother. She wanted one of my mop dolls that I created and made my own pattern. It was a Rabbit with a dress. They were beautiful, and I got lots of compliments on them. I found the Clown in a magazine and altered the pattern. After I made the Spice-colored Clowns, I started making Spice-colored toaster covers. And the little sheep I made were so Adorable. I made a doll from my Grandma Grace's doll pattern and gave it to my Niece. I wish I could have made more to look like that one, but the others didn't seem to turn out as nice.

I later started working in Corvallis Clinic. I would go visit my best friend that worked in Corvallis Clinic. She asked me if I would like to work there. I started the next week. I really only wanted a part-time job, but ended up working full-time and a lot of overtime. I worked as a file clerk, and she allowed me to create my own way of doing things. I had to be very careful about filing the charts because it could have meant life or death for a patient if the chart was not found for their Appointments. I enjoyed working for my friend. The charts would come down the chute in the chart room and would be put on carts to be filed. Then my boss decided to have them put on the carts at each floor. That is when the problems started. Each cart weighed over 300 pounds, and this made it very difficult for me to maneuver. My friend moved on to a different job in the Clinic, and we got a new Supervisor. I didn't seem to get along with her so well. But she would come to me and ask me for ideas on how we could improve the Records department. I would tell her my ideas, and she would tell me how they wouldn't work and then later implement them. I soon learned her trickery and stopped giving her ideas, because she would never give me the credit but take the credit for herself. I kept telling her that they needed to *change the pickup of charts on the carts back to the way it was, but she did not listen. I told her someone was going to get hurt. Not knowing that person was going to be me. There were times that I had to actually lift the cart to get into the elevator. I hurt my back and could not do that any longer. I put in an Accident report and was betrayed by my own Doctor that took her side. I was put on light duty. I should have just not worked because I didn't even get Workman's Comp. She didn't even give me my Christmas bonus. The reason, she said, is because they were doing a point system and I was one point off. That was mean on her part. She let the Assistant Supervisor tell me. I put up with her shenanigans till I had to have a Hysterectomy, and I never went back. I later found out that I was replaced by a man and he was being paid three times what I made. Even though I should have gotten a raise, she would not give it to me. Before I left, I had the job I should have had from the beginning. I answered the phone and got to talk to the Nurses and Doctors. I was able to calm down the Doctors when they were upset about not getting the chart that they needed. Sometimes everyone would have to look through every single chart to find the right one. I heard after I left that the girls would tell my replacement, "Just wait till Margene is back." I didn't even know that any of them liked me, because of how they would stand around and talk about me. Oh well, another chapter of my life ended, and I am still thankful to this day that I did not go back.*

My Girls!

July 29, 2015 at 8:03am

My first baby has been in Heaven before she even had a chance to breathe outside of the Womb. I got really sick and think I had walking pneumonia. I was so sick I thought I was dying. I did not want my baby to die, but that is what happened. So I called the Doctor. At that time I could call him personally, and he told me I needed to come into the Clinic. I sat in the waiting room waiting to be seen and then I heard them say my name and that I had left. I almost ran to the desk and said, "I did not leave, I am right here." They took me back to the room. It was so cold and sterile. The doctor could no longer hear the baby's heartbeat. With tears streaming down my face, my heart sank. I had already loved the little baby inside of me that I wanted to name after my brother Dan. Dapper Dan, I affectionately called him. I wanted to name her Danielle. I knew she would have Black hair and Blue eyes. Anyway, that is how I envisioned her. I knew she would be beautiful, because her daddy is half Japanese and so handsome and my Sister-in-Law is so Beautiful. And I saw pics of my Mother-in-Law when she was younger. Such a beauty.

But my heart broke when they told me that I would have to go to the Hospital to have a D&C. I did not even know what that really meant. I just knew that she had to come out of my body, or I would get an infection. My body would be poisoned by own baby!

I lay there in disbelief. I could not believe it. Was this a nightmare I was having.

In the Hospital, they took a long needle and inserted into my stomach and took some of the Amniotic Fluid to make sure the baby was not living. And then they gave me something to induce labor for her to come out. I lay there in shock and could feel all the emotions in my body. The little life that I harbored and kept protected inside of me was going to come out and not be living, not alive. I was feeling guilt because I had felt so sick, I just wanted to die, but not my baby. Not my baby!

The nurses came into to see me from time to time to see if I needed anything and to check on my progress. I asked the nurse if I could have some tissue, and she gave it to me. The Doctor came in later and asked me about it and then got upset with the Nurse, saying, "Don't you realize that she could get an infection from the contamination of the tissue?" Wow, that is crazy that she would not even know that. But she was just trying to help.

Then I started to feel the contractions and they said, "Push, push!" And then the baby came out. The Doctor said, "It is a girl." I wanted to see her, but the Doctor told me no. No, why not? He said she was perfect. I wondered why he didn't want me to see her, but I did not question or even insist on seeing her. I trusted this Doctor and thought he knew best.

I was there alone. Only my husband came and saw me. I wanted my own Mommy to come and comfort me. I wanted my Sister-in-Law, but I felt so alone and wondering why I was going through this all alone.

I did not know that my husband was feeling guilty, because he had taken drugs when he was in the Army and then kept drinking after he was out. The guilt that he was the cause of this Tragedy lay heavily on him.

Inside both our minds, the devil was having a heyday trying to make us feel guilty.

Why didn't Danielle want to come into life on Earth? I began to think. Why did she change her mind? Did she know something I did not know?

Then it was time for me to go home. I was supposed to go home with a little bundle of joy. Not with just memories of what could or should have been. I hurt not only physically, but my emotions ran in a torrent. Crying at anything. Was my Faith being tested? I still loved God no matter what, and I knew that my little Danielle was in Heaven with others in my Family that had gone on before her. And with HIM and that HE was holding her close to HIS HEART so she could HEAR HIS HEARTBEAT and be comforted and feel LOVED.

Life goes on whether you want it to or not, and about a month or so later, the Doctor told us that we could try again. And miraculously I got pregnant again, and I had a beautiful little girl. I loved her from the beginning and would sing and talk to her even before she came into the World. I taught her about Jesus like my mom taught me. And then three years later, I had another baby girl. My daughter, Kelly, was fair. So funny because my Mother-in-law was sure she would be darker and look Japanese.

And then when April came along, she had Dark hair and black eyes. Both a beautiful combination of what God put in both their Daddy and me. God gave me the family I always wanted. Not saying it was easy, but I loved my Daughters with all of my Heart. They were my Life, my gift from God. It was funny. For years, I always felt that someone was missing. Almost like Danielle was there. I think Kelly even said something one time to me about feeling like someone else was there.

I often wondered if babies are looking down from Heaven and saying, "I want to go to that family." I wondered why Danielle had to go back.

Oh, the Doctor that delivered April said, "You are made to have babies." I did not want to have more, but I would have loved to Adopt, but my husband did not want to adopt, but to just have our own.

Protecting Life!

Thursday, October 20, 2016

I have seen the devastation of losing a child. I did not have an Abortion, but I have talked to women that have and know their guilt and the haunting that they experience. I know my child is in Heaven and believe that all that were aborted are in Heaven. (After I had to go into the Hospital to have a D&C to have the baby removed. At the appointment after this, the Nurse Practitioner asked me why I had an Abortion. Very sad, because I had to tell her my baby died inside of me and had to have it removed. She was so embarrassed and apologized over and over. She should have read my file. Would have saved face. And would have saved me from the hurt I felt.) I could argue this until I am blue in the face. It is so inhumane the way they murder these babies. How is this different than protecting toddlers? Or should I say *not protecting toddlers*. Guns are our right as Americans. Education, and putting them in a place where children can't get them. Use wisdom. I do agree we need to know that we are not selling to murderers and reckless people. Oh, wow I could go on and on, but you get my drift. My point being is that these children have had their rights taken away from them. I am glad I did not have to make a choice if my child came into this World. It is like she said, "I changed my mind. I want to go back to Heaven, where I know I will be safe and loved." I will someday find out, but for now I am satisfied and thankful she is in Heaven and I will someday see her again. I don't have to carry around that guilt of an Abortion and do believe that women that do can ask for forgiveness. But it is time to think about it and choose other ways to prevent an unwanted Pregnancy. Like choosing to give your baby to a loving home, etc. If every child is considered a blessing, then why would we as Christians condone abortion? My heart cries for all the Children that have been aborted, but is broken thinking of all the ones that will be aborted in the future. The other night I watched Texas Rangers. Yup, I watch this with my Dad, but actually like Westerns myself. Great learning tools. He said there are consequences to every action. We are seeing the consequences of many who chose to have sex, so will you take responsibility for what you did or try to hide it? Or will you allow the consequence to be a beautiful child that could grow up to be the next Billy Graham or Joyce Meyers? Or, or, or... If it is true that God Our Father knew us before the foundation of the World, before we were in our Mother's Womb, Do we really have the right to abandon HIS plan for their life? I am not trying to cause trouble but to make people think. TRUTH TIME! I WANT TO SPEAK UP FOR THOSE THAT WERE NOT EVEN GIVEN A CHANCE TO SPEAK. You don't have to agree, but you do need to respectful to me and to others that come on my page. Love in JESUS. TO OUR FATHER, ALL OF THE GLORY!

Art Classes

I wanted to take some Art Classes, but my husband did not want me to. But I stood up to him and told him that if he could go hunting and fishing and leave me home to take care of our girls, he could watch them while I did something I enjoyed. I went to classes with my neighbor, and we did oil painting and she then took up tole painting and began teaching classes herself. I later changed teachers. I became good friends with my second teacher, and when she married another painter, she invited me to the Wedding. It was so much fun.

Mom Goes to Heaven

June of 1985

I always called my Mom, and we would always say "I love you" to each other at the end of each call. My Mom was living in Port Charlotte, Florida. She originally went there by herself but was later joined by my cousin Cheryl. I missed her so much and wanted to be near her. But I was Married with two small children.

I had planned on going to see her but at that time had a fear of Flying. Come on now, I was *going to become an Airline Hostess after I graduated from High School. At that time, I actually wanted to be a Model, but that was not to be. I was going to Weaver School that you could do most of it at home. You need to have a lot of self-control to do home schooling. Since I didn't, I did not finish.*

I had called Mom, and she had been given a New medication that she said would be out of her system in about a month. She had just been at a place that was checking her out for her Pituitary Gland. I told her they were using her like a Guinea pig, and we had a big laugh about that. They were checking her out, and she actually seemed to enjoy it there. She was able to do crafts there. She made Indian dream catchers and a variety of other things. She made friends with some of the other patients. They were upset with the Clinic that she had in Oregon, because she should have had Surgery on her Pituitary but decided against it. The Gland is a gland that controls everything in your body. She had several heart attacks and other problems throughout her life because of it. She aged quickly, and her face got distorted. So after she went back home, the Doctors tried a new medication on her. I was talking to her on the phone, and she said that the medication was not working, but she would be fine when it was out of her system. It was upsetting to me to know that they had given her such a drug. She had told me that the Pharmacist had told her that a lot of the medications that she took were not meant to be taken together. So why did he give them to her? My Mom was a smart woman, but she still listened to the Doctors. So then we waited. I was in Oregon, and she was in Florida. Even though she always said we were only a phone call away, when she was sick, that phone call did not help. She would say to me, "I sure wish you would come and see me," but did not say, "You need to come see me."

So time went by, and she was not getting any better. I then got a call from my Sister telling me that she just took Mom to the Hospital. I asked why she waited so long, and she said, "Because Mom wanted Dad to take her." What! I could not believe that Mom was waiting for Dad to take her. It made me feel sick because I was not there with my Mom that I loved so much. The woman who taught me about Jesus from a young age. The woman that always said "I love you, Margene" at the end of each phone call.

I had called her at the Hospital and just had told her "I Love you, Mom" and then heard myself say, "Hang up the phone, Mom," not knowing that would be our last phone call. I felt so guilty for telling her that. But what was going on? The Doctor had said she was doing fine. But that was the Emergency Room Doctor. What happened when her Doctor came back? Where was the caring? For God's sake, she was only fifty-nine years old. She still had a lot of life to live. Then came the phone call that I dreaded. Hearing my Dad say, "Margene, your Mom is gone."

I said, "Dad, did you tell her that the boys and I are coming to see her?"

He said, "Yes, I told her."

I was so angry I told my brothers that I was not going.

"Margene, you need to go for Dad."

"No, I am not going." I was so angry with everyone at that point. Couldn't Mom hold on till we got there? I wanted to pray for her. Now realizing that when you go to Heaven, you get your healing. I was numb. We drove up to Portland, Oregon, and got on the Airplane. I ended up paying at least double the price than if I would have gone a month before. My neighbor told me earlier if it was her Mom, she would spend any amount to go. So at this point, it did not matter how much it cost. At least I was not going alone. I had my brothers with me. Leaving my little family not to go visit with my Mom but to go to a Funeral, the first Funeral I ever went to. I cried all the way there. I know my brothers were hurting too. We were all in our own little Worlds of Grief. I wanted to be with my Mom so bad, but knew I had two little girls that needed me. I did not want to commit Suicide, but the longing to just be with her was just so strong.

At the Funeral, I went up to the Coffin, and it was not my Mother, but a stranger seemed to be lying there. Knowing that she was already out of her body. She didn't look like my mom. There was no life left for me to see that it was her. Her hair was almost all white, and her makeup did not look good. I think I tried to fix it, but putting makeup on someone that is no longer there is very difficult. I gave her a kiss on her forehead, but it was so strange. She was stiff and not warm and soft like she was when she was living. I went back to my seat. Somehow, I wished that I could just remember her when she was my Mom instead of lying there cold and stiff and alone. Thankfully, I kept reminding myself about the Bible verse that said, "Absent from the body, Present with the Lord." I also kept reminding myself I would see her again one day, so why was I so sad. Knowing now that when someone leaves us to go to Heaven, they would not want to come back. It is us that are selfish to wish they were still here. Being in Heaven should be our ultimate goal. We are truly Home.

Mom joined an Indian tribe in Florida, and they gave her the name Little White Elk. They came to the viewing and later did part of the Service. It was so beautiful. One of the Indians told me that when they talk about the sun, they are actually talking about Jesus. One of them told me there was lot of Hawks around that meant she was watching over us. I was thankful they came that day and many others. Her family came, and that made me happy. So funny, Mom's oldest sister asked me if Mom loved Jesus. I was dumbfounded to think my Aunt didn't know her own sister loved Jesus so much. Even though Mom loved Jesus, she still wanted to live. I think she knew we would have a hard time without her. That is the thing, our loved ones go on to a better place, which is in Heaven, and we are left here missing them. My Mom was in pain, so I would not want her to come back, but at that time I really wanted to be with her. I was so thankful that God let me talk to her whenever I wanted to. It would take a long time to adjust, and for a long time, I kept thinking she was only a Phone call away.

Back Home with My Little Family

Flying back home, I was still numb and couldn't stop thinking about my Mom, and I still wanted to be with her but reminded myself that I had two little girls that I loved so much, and they needed me. I did not realize that they were dealing with their own loss of their Grandmother. My daughter April later told me about seeing my Mom in a vision visiting with her. I sometimes thought how my girls missed out so much on being with their Grandma 'cause even when she lived close, she could not have them very often because of her health; she was not strong enough to take care of two girls.

But we were going to make it through. I cannot say that time takes away all the pain that you go through, but our lives had to go on. I know Mom would have wanted it to be that way.

I had missed them so much and even missed my husband. You know the saying "Absence makes the Heart grow fonder." The years went by so quickly. I still think of my Mom so often. But realizing she is in Heaven, I know that she is still doing the things that she loves, like writing and Art. And what a rush to know that she gets to talk to not only Jesus, but to all the people that have gone on before her and gets to meet the new ones at the Gate to welcome them Home.

I am coming someday soon to see you too. Give my Danielle a hug for me and all my precious critters, including my Horse, Adia Bador. I love you, Mom.

Working at the Farm Home and Being a Teacher Assistant

I went to the Employment Office to check out jobs, and the woman working with me sent me to the School District. They were having a job fair. The woman wanted me to put in for a Clerical Job in the School office. So I put in for that job, but then they asked if there were any people that wanted to put in for Teacher Assistant positions. I raised my hand, not thinking if I was really even qualified for that job. But there was something intriguing about working with kids in that way. Working alongside teachers. I saw it as a way of helping. To my Amazement, I was called a few days later for a position, taking the place of a teacher assistant that was struggling with her health. She worked with the Special-needs students. How Ironic! So I went in and started the next day. Everyone was so nice. It was at a Middle School. Wow, I was on my way. I loved helping not only the Teachers but the students as well. Mainly the students needed encouragement. One boy was actually smarter than he put on, and I told him to start acting like he was smart. I actually went and saw him a year later in High School, and he was an A student and on the Honor Roll.

I got to be in that job for quite a while, then the woman came back and I was moved to another School and another grade. I worked with a lot of kids, some in the regular classrooms and some in Special Education. From Kindergarten up to Seniors, I loved them all, and they seemed to love me too. The ones I had the hardest times with were the ones with physical handicaps, because some had brilliant minds but were in bodies that did not function right. I would almost have nightmares about those kids because I felt so bad for them.

While at the Schools, I was told that I could not hug the kids or talk about Jesus. The amazing thing is that I found books in the cupboard that were based on the Bible. I was elated to know that those were the textbooks that the School used to use to teach the students.

Then I started being called by the Farm Home that had children that could not live at home with their parents for one reason or another. They became my favorite group of kids. I worked mainly with the boys, and a lot of them had mental issues.

I had just got trained on how to take care of different situations, like putting the kids down on the ground if they were getting out of hand. I didn't seem to have any problems like that with the kids there. They all seemed to respect me, and therefore I respected them. After we got trained, we went back to the classroom, and we were all walking back to the house the kids lived in and one of the boys asked me if he could go on ahead. If I would have known what was going to happen when I got back there, I would not have giving him permission to go. He ran ahead, and a woman that had just gone through the training with me asked me if I gave him permission, and before I could answer her, she was putting him down and asking me to help her. Before I could even get there, the boy flipped me, putting his foot in back of my foot and flipping me onto my back. I was so mad at that woman. Not at the boy, he didn't deserve to be put down. He asked me, and I gave him permission. I talked to the teacher I was working with and told him what happened. I told him that I was there to assist him in teaching not to physically put the students down. He agreed, and I never had to do that again.

I also went to work at a House that they had in town. I got to work with students that were far smarter than me. One student was a math whiz and was doing math that I never learned. We did the classwork down in the basement and came upstairs to have lunch. I got to help them make cookies one time, and that was fun. The boys were very respectful.

Back at the Farm Home, I became good friends with a woman that also worked there. Even though she was single and I was married, we did things together. My husband didn't seem to mind. I found out later what he really thought of it, and it was not very nice at all. I got to work a lot as a Teacher Assistant, and it is written down in my Memory book as one of my favorite jobs.

The Years Go By

The years went by Fast and Furious. Sometimes so disturbing that it was crazy how fast the years were gone and no way of slowing them down. My girls grew to be more beautiful and determined to become their own women. Not that everything was perfect. Quite the contrary. But that is their stories to tell.

But my heart was broken when My oldest moved to another State just a few days before my first Grandson's birthday. And then after my Divorce, she was not ready for me to come there to visit. And then my youngest moved to be near her. I was so happy that they would be near each other. Sisters need each other.

What Led Up to Getting a Divorce?

Unbelievable, she was such a pretty little Italian Woman and had a sweet little baby. The first time we met, a friend brought me to see her. I was very Depressed and not a very happy person. Disillusioned with my Marriage. Not believing in Psychics but at that time, I did not know what to do. She said that she was getting her information from God, so I listened to her when she told me that I was unhappy and needed to get out of my Marriage. I thought I was there to convert her and bring her to Love Jesus. I kept telling her that she needed to use her gift for God and become a Prophet. I became friends with her, and she trusted me. She even asked me to come and stay with her when her husband went out of town. I could not believe that she was afraid to be alone.

She kept telling me that I needed to get a Divorce and that the man I was supposed to Marry was waiting for me. I listened but was not convinced yet that was what God wanted me to do. I kept praying, asking HIM what HE wanted me to do. Then there it was, the Answer to what I was to do, Not from her, but it was there in Black and White that my husband did not love me. His true feelings about me so plain. My Release from Marriage was all there. The Answer to my Prayer all written out. I called the Psychiatrist and asked if my life was in danger. She told me that she was not supposed to tell me under normal circumstances, but since my life could be in danger, she felt she needed to tell me the truth. She then proceeded and told me it was true and that I should make sure that I got rid of all guns and knives. I called my brother and asked if I could keep all guns and knives at his house. The weird thing was that my husband and I were actually getting along okay, but we had the worst fight we ever had when I presented him with the letter and asked him for a Divorce. I also told him not to ask me to stay with him.

I let my little Italian friend know that I was going to get a Divorce and had it in process. She no longer told me that I would soon meet the man I was supposed to be with and later told me that, that man would not come for years. Today I wonder if she actually put a curse on me, because I have been single again for many years. I truly liked that woman, but I was thankful when she moved away and I did not see her anymore. I do not know if she ever became a Christian. I planted the seeds, but also asked Abba Father for forgiveness for going to see her in the first place. I am not sorry I got a Divorce, because I think all that happened was used to release me from an Unloving relationship. I truly wanted both of us to be with the people we were truly meant to be with. I hold nothing against her and do not hold anything against my ex-husband. I still long to be Married to the one that Abba Father has for me.

Sometimes I have wondered why my ex could not love me the way I longed to be loved, but then why could I not love him the way he needed to be loved? Then I realize that if I did not Divorce him, I would have not learned all that I learned to go Forward to do Abba's work for HIS Kingdom. I would not have gone on the Mission Trips, met the people I now know. I would be trapped in a small town and still yearning to be Free. Like the Dream I had about a bird being in a bird cage, and one day the door was left open out on a Porch, and the bird flew out of the cage into freedom. I now know that bird was me. Now I want to Soar like an Eagle Above the Clouds, going where the Lord leads me.

I will continue to pray for that little Italian woman, that she follows Jesus, and for my ex, that He follows Jesus too. Finding that Forgiveness is not always forgetting what happened but being healed so that you can talk about what happened without hurting anymore.

Chapter 5

Divorce

Indecision, Decision

2010

It's confusing when you're trying to make a decision that is going to change your life forever. When you finally make that decision and stick with it, it is like having the feeling of complete triumph—that a weight like a two-ton elephant has been lifted off your shoulders. The sticking with it is the hard part, especially when you have friends and family that don't want you to change. When I decided to get a divorce, so much life got in the way that it took years to finally go through with the process. Was it life or fear? Being afraid of losing my children. Wow, what a revelation. I had forced that one back into the storage banks of my mind. You know the part where you put things you really don't what to deal with because to deal with them would be far too painful? My kids were my life. Afraid that I would be making a huge mistake, because he really was a pretty good guy, wasn't he? Just because my self-esteem was non-existent and just because I felt no one else would love and accept me the way I was like he did. He needed me. I was there to help him, save him. Save him from what? Being an alcoholic? From self-destructing? Combusting and going completely mad? Going through Milestones Alcohol Treatment Center with him was pure Hell for me. Having to listen to how bad he felt for all his other girlfriends in how he had treated them. What about me? Wasn't I the one who was his wife and the mother of his children? For God's sake! What about me? Thank God! He finally sought the help of the VA (Veterans) to help him get over the hurdle of being in Vietnam. I did not want to even try to fathom the horror of being in a war that no one wanted to support, let alone come to terms with, and acknowledge that it really happened, but like the alcohol treatment, I stuck with him through all the pain of flashbacks, and nightmares, the sad whimpering like a sad puppy when he was having a nightmare. Waking him, assuring him that it was only a bad dream and that no one was chasing him. I didn't want to hear what the dream was about because I didn't want to relive his horror in my own dreams What I found is no one can save you; you must save yourself. Once I found that truth, the decision to get a divorce was easy. Besides, I needed to save myself, and I wouldn't be able to do that in the confines of and unhealthy, unloving marriage. Inside ourselves, we have an image, and ideal of what a happy marriage should look like, and my marriage didn't even come close to my internal perception of what that would be. The worst thing about being in a bad relationship is that you can't give your children a good example of what a good, loving, healthy relationship should look and feel like. I guess that my biggest regret about not making the decision sooner is that I could have possibly gotten into a healthy relationship. It seemed every time I tried to get out of the marriage before, my children would talk me into staying. They would do this even though they were the ones that would tell me, "Divorce dad because he's so mean to you." Wow! what the human heart does to contradict itself to stay in the familiar. Love has always been important to me, and I always wondered why I couldn't love this man, but how easy it was to love the children we created together. I yearned to be with my soul mate and came to the tearful conclusion that this man wasn't him. Not only was I sad for myself at this revelation, but I was sad for him because I knew he deserved to be with someone that loved and cherished him. I knew I could no longer try to be that person, and I knew I deserved the same for myself. It's amazing how the minutes, hours, and oh yes, the years just pass in a blink of an eye. A speck of time in the scheme of things. Here I was at my wedding not knowing if I was doing the right thing. Even though I had a gut-wrenching feeling that I should not be going through with it, but then I said to myself, "If it happens, it must be meant to be." A decision not to make a decision is the worst decision of all, because the decision usually turns out to be the wrong one. That feeling long ago while standing in front of the minister when God was telling me I shouldn't marry this man. Maybe He was really telling me, "This is just a small part of your life," because if I hadn't gone through with the marriage, I wouldn't have had two beautiful daughters and a beautiful grandson that took twenty-one years to come into existence. What could be more gratifying than bringing life to children that could possibly make all your wrong decisions right just by being? So why did God give us a brain anyway just to let life happen to us, or for us to make our lives the best we can? Now I know it is our duty as human beings to use the intelligence God gave us to make good decisions. If we really listen, He will even help us. It may be that gut-wrenching feeling, a friendly word whispered in our ear, a gentle tug at a corner of our heart, or that nagging little thought that runs helter-skelter through the recesses of our minds. Life is a learning experience. I hope I learned what I needed to learn, and now I have a second chance. Not a chance to go back and change the past, but the chance to change the future into something that I can be proud of. Regrets are futile and not worth my energy. I am ready to fulfill my destiny;

I hope I will do something that will leave a loving imprint on all humanity. Or at least I know that from now on my decisions will be the right decisions, so I can continue my saga of life in dignity.

No One Is to Blame for Getting a Divorce

(I want to clarify that I did not Divorce him, because of my Children. On the contrary. I Divorced him because I felt for my own safety, I needed to and that Abba Father released me.) I do not hold any ill will toward my ex and want him to be happy and find the person who will love him the way he needs to be loved. That letter I found was from twenty years ago. I have moved on, and I know he has moved on. It is funny how many people said there is someone else out there for me, but the man has not come forward yet. But I am still believing that HE has someone for me because HE is the Promise Keeper.

Chapter 6

Getting a Second Chance

In March of 1999, we were getting a Divorce. Unbelievable but true, my husband and I was at the Courthouse. I got the papers and had filled them out and asked him to pay for the Divorce. Pretty good deal for him because I was not asking for anything but my Freedom. Freedom was worth more to me than anything. I had watched both of my brothers getting Divorces, and seeing what they went through with their ex-wives and feeling bad for them, I did not want to put my soon to be ex-husband through such treachery. Not knowing that he was not going to be so kind to me. But here we were and filling out some more papers, and the only thing that was going to be divided was the sale of the house. At that time, I was living in the house. I loved that house, but I wrote I would keep it unless he wanted to sell it. Was that foolish on my part, because of course, he wanted to sell it. So the Judge signed the Divorce, and we were no longer Married.

The House went on the Market. I asked the Real Estate woman that found a buyer for our house on Highway 20. During that time, I went to the Dentist to get some work done, and he gave me a numbing shot in the back of my mouth, and then I went home and woke up the next morning. I looked in the mirror and my mouth, my eye was drooping. Thinking I had a Stroke, I had my daughter take me to the Emergency Room. The Doctors assured me that I did not have a Stroke but that I had Bell's Palsy, and I wondered if I was being punished for getting a Divorce! My daughter told my ex-husband, and he came to the Hospital. I was so embarrassed and asked him why he was there. I was not very nice but did not want him to see me with a drooping face. He was no longer my husband. I did not want his sympathy—worse yet, his Pity. I don't know what he thought but was glad that he left. Here was something else I would be going through alone. While at the Hospital, they gave me something that was supposed to help get rid of the Palsy right away. They told me it would go away on its own, not telling that I should not sleep by a window or let a fan blow on me. I did both, and I would dream that I was okay and that my Smile was back, but I would look in the mirror the next day and the nightmare was still there. I went to the Doctor, and she did nothing that really helped me. She was supposed to get therapy for me and get me vitamin B Shots for the Nerves. I know I was healed from it. While all this was going on and being sick, I still had to try to keep the house clean so people could look at the house. I had no one helping me. I was thankful for my daughter being there, but she was busy with other things.

My Real Estate woman was supposed to be working for me not knowing that she was really working on my ex's behalf. She was telling me to list everything I needed to be paid for but telling him the same thing. We were supposed to get an even fifty-fifty, and he ended up getting more. What the hay, I was being stolen from again! Not only was the enemy trying to take my looks from me, he was also working through my Real Estate woman, trying to steal my money. I was trying to do the right thing by my ex not asking for what I rightfully deserved, but my kindness was being brutally taken advantage of by not even getting half of the sale of the house. She had reduced the price of the house, but he did not care; he just wanted to not let me keep it.

Years later, I look back and see how God did not want me to stay there but to move me Forward in the Direction HE wanted me to go.

Apparently, HE did not want me to be a Model either. So, Lord, What do YOU want me to do?

Chapter 7

New Beginnings in Florida

Moving On

The house was sold, and it was time to think of what I was going to do next. A friend told me that I could come and stay with her while I was figuring things out. I got a little bit of money from the house and needed a car and a new home. I had told my youngest daughter that she could have my car. I just didn't realize she thought I meant right then.

I had been going to the Consortium in Corvallis, Oregon, and I was told that they wanted me to interview for a job. Wow, they thought more of me than I thought of myself. But the woman I was staying with was getting weary of me staying there. She had a lot of problems that I did not realize she had, so she said that her counselor told her that she needed to ask me to move. So I said okay and was praying where I should go. I felt that the Father was asking me to write down some destinations, because even though I was looking at houses locally, I was not seeing anything I liked. One house had some steep steps to the front door that freaked me out, and none of the other places were even close to what I had. So I wrote down four places: California, Arizona, Georgia, and Florida. California was where my Aunt and Uncle lived. The door was slammed shut. Arizona, my brother had a Mobile home there. The door was slammed shut because he no longer had it. Georgia, the door was closed because my daughter was not ready to have me come. She was just getting her little family together. My sister in Florida said I could go there. Door opened wide. I had a dream before she told me that I was in Sarasota and looking around. The thing was that when I got to Florida, that was where I went and thought I should have stayed at one of the Hotels, but I called my sister, and she came and picked me up. I sometimes wonder what turn my life would have taken if I had stayed there. You know those Woulda, Coulda, Shoulda Moments. C'est la vie.

Train
Grandma and a Man We Called Doc
(This is a Short Story I came up with about moving to Florida. Most of it is true.)

As I entered the train station in Albany, Oregon, my eyes automatically focused on an older gentleman. If he wasn't a man, I would have sworn my grandmother had come back to take this life-changing trip with me, but she was in Heaven. It did cause the memories of the long-ago trips of my youth to see her and her husband we all called Doc.

It would always be the same scenario. Dad would come home on Fridays after a long hard working day at his Saw Filing Shop, where he sharpened big saws for the local lumber mills in Philomath, Oregon, and a few on the outskirts of the town.

His announcement was always, "Hurry up and get ready. We're going to see Grandma." Before we could go, we had to make sure the house was cleaned up. That kind of ruined the spontaneity of the trip, but it didn't ruin the excitement of going. We always made sure the house was spotless, because Mom would remind us that nothing was worse than coming home to a dirty house, and it was a nice to slip into clean crisp sheets after the long drive home. I could never figure how it always seemed like it took forever to get to a place and just half the time to get home.

Off we went for the drive that seemed to always bring up the same question over and over again: "Are we there yet?" With the resounding same answer, "Not yet, but it won't be long now."

We would finally get there after what seemed like an eternity, even though we had slept most of the way, in between the squabbling that sisters and brothers do because they're bored out of their gourd.

Grandma and Doc, and sometimes my Uncle John, would come out to greet us with gigantic grins on their faces. They seemed just as excited to see us as we were in seeing them. We seemed to fall out of the car because we had "car lag" from being confined for far too long, but being kids, we didn't feel the effects long.

The first thing we wanted to do was see the goats, and we hoped for some new baby kids to pet. Doc always had a fun way to call them, and I swear he sounded just like one of them. Baaaaaa! BAAAA! BAAAA!

It seemed we were starving by the time we got there, so we anxiously went into the house, which always had the scent of Grandma in every nook and cranny. Not a sweet smell, or even a sour citrus smell, but a unique Grandma smell that made us feel all warm inside because if we could smell that fragrance, we knew that we were loved.

Grandma's smell had to compete with the sensational smells of the roast beef cooking in the oven. It always had fresh carrots, potatoes, onions, garlic right out of the garden depending on what time of the year it was. If we were lucky, Uncle John gathered mushrooms in the woods that morning. It was a delight to our noses as the juices combined to entice us with their luscious fragrance that had been simmering most of the day. Then the tantalizing bread that had just been baked, fresh from the oven, a combination of nuts, different grains, anything Grandma could think of that would make her bread unique, and flavorful. It was always crispy on the outside, tender on the inside, generously sliced with gobs of goat's butter and possibly cheese, sweet honey, and even homemade strawberry, or blueberry jam, if the mood hit us to explore our taste buds.

Of course, there was always ice-cold goat's milk, and Doc always proposed the question, "Do you like goat's milk?" and we gave the resounding answer: "Yeeeeeeeees!" We were pretty good imitators, but Doc had taught us this from the first time we met. For dessert, we weren't quite sure if we'd like it because Grandma always experimented with the goat's milk. She tried her hand at ice cream and sometimes came up with some pretty strange concoctions. Sometimes we didn't even know what to say because we didn't want to hurt her feelings, but yuck! Some of it was gross, and we couldn't even eat it without having an uncontrollable urge to upchuck. Sometimes, though, she'd come up with something good, like peach ice cream, so we'd try it even though we knew that we might be making a mistake.

After we were totally stuffed, and wanting to roll out the door, because our stomachs seemed to moan "you fed me far too much," my two brothers, sister, and I would go outside to have a little adventure of our own while the grownups stayed in the house to visit.

Adventures on Grandma's farm were fun for us because not living on a farm, we could roam freely without the confines of streets and concrete sidewalks. The dirt was either hot or cool depending on whether we were under numerous trees in the woods or standing in an open field. We had to watch out for the stinky old Billy goat because we were warned that he liked to butt you. The rank, putrid old goat had horns, too, so we didn't want to test his ornery moods by getting in his area of the pasture. We hoped some kind of fence was between him and us, protecting our tender backsides.

Doc sometimes came out with us because he liked to tell us stories of the good ole days when he grew up and his adventures as a traveling salesman. We never tired of his stories because he told a story so entertainingly that we felt we were there wherever there was. His stories were better than fairy tales because we knew they were real, and it made us closer every time he shared another little part of himself with us.

My favorite story he would tell us is about his family living in a small cabin in the woods at the bottom of Mount St. Helens. The farmers and town folk nicknamed old Mount St. Helens "Madcap" because they never knew when she would blow. The mountain was festering up something, because every once in a while, people would say they could hear her rumbling and making all sorts of weird noises. Stories abounded how the *volcano would erupt again someday. Doc told of this old man named Truman that swore he would never leave even if Old Madcap blew. Doc told us about his sister Anne, who sat on the fence gate and yodeled to her audience of cows and a bull named King Alfred. Her ambition in life was to grow up and be a cowgirl and ride in the rodeos. His parents gave Doc his nickname because he nursed every sick animal back to health. He had that special combination of love and intuition that gave him the insight to know exactly what kind of herbs would cure the poor critters. One day, a traveling salesman came by his family's cabin selling different concoctions promising to cure anything from the common cold to Scarlet Fever. The man had everything on his wagon that a person would ever need. From that day, Doc decided that, that is what he wanted to be. He began dreaming from that day of the adventures that he would be traveling from town to town. He told us that it disappointed his parents, but his dreams would come true. It sure made good stories to tell us—his grandchildren.*

All aboard. It was time to go. I grabbed my bags and took my little girl Charlie (Chihuahua) and put her under my arm and boarded the train. It was time to start my adventure. Doc would be proud. I knew that throughout the trip to Florida, I would continue to visit memory lane where I would meet Grandma and the man we called Doc.

Living in St. Pete

Posted by Sunwhisp
11:52 a.m.

I lived with my Niece. One day she said, Auntie Margene, I don't like to see you so lonely. I am going to sign you up for a dating service. She found a local one in St. Petersburg, Florida. They gave me the name Sunwhisp, and it stuck. I loved that name. I started having men contact me, and my niece and her boyfriend would take me to meet these men at a bookstore in the mall. They would chaperone at a distance. Some men showed up and some didn't. Some were more memorable than others. One in particular came and was wearing a T-Shirt with a big ship on it, and he wore some ragity tennis shoes. I was so turned off, but he invited me to go to the Beach by where he lived. My niece and her boyfriend went also. It was so beautiful, and since it was Fourth of July it was spectacular seeing the Fireworks. The thing was I could not stand him even holding my hand, and when he tried to kiss *me that was it, I decided I really did not like to date.*

Then I was talking to this one guy that I was really becoming friends with. I didn't have a picture yet and the picture he had was a man with a young boy. One day he finally decided to take me out and he was going to come pick me up. I was sitting at my computer in front of the window. The window was the total front of the Apartment. A chubby little man walked by the window, and I watched him walk to the door. He knocked at the door and I went and opened it, and I asked the man at the door who he was...He said Margene I am Antonio. (Antonio is my favorite name, so this man started calling himself Antonio.) My mouth must have fallen open. I asked him to come in. He came in and then all of a sudden, he said, I need to go and make a phone call. He went to his pickup and then I heard a vehicle speed away. I later called him and asked why he lied to me. Ok let me tell you why I was shocked. Because of the picture. The man was tall and handsome. I figured out after he came to see me that the man was his dad, and he was the little boy in the picture. The thing is we were friends. And if he would have told me the truth, I would like to think I would have hung out with him anyway. But because he lied to me there was no chance of that happening.

I am such a glutton for punishment. I started talking to this one man and agreed to meet him at a Pool parlor in another city. I had a car at that my point, so I agreed to meet him there. (I told myself I would never do that again.) I went there and I met him. That man had lied about his age. I asked him why he lied, and he said, I figured you probably lied. I did not. I still did not have a picture, so had to describe myself. We did play pool, and then I went home. I had fun, but never saw him again. And the reason he did not come to me was he only rode a bicycle.

Honesty or Reality versus Fantasy
2011

Being a writer, I can manufacture in my mind what I would like in a Relationship. To bring it into existence takes a little more effort. The problem with a fantasy is that is all it is—a Fantasy. No matter how you look at it, it isn't reality.

Being on the Internet, a lot of relationships can take place, but they are not real until you meet face-to-face. So you can say that you love that person all you want, but if you never meet and nothing will go any further, you will never get married. You will never have children with that person, if that is your desire. You will never have a physical touch. Emotionally you may be sucked in, but that is all there is to the relationship. Raw emotion that can only cause you mental anguish.

It is amazing to me that I myself can get caught up in what is really a game to some of these men that are on the Internet. They barely come on Facebook, let's say, and they seem to seek me out. I almost feel like I have a bull's-eye on my forehead. Come speak to me, I will believe your baloney. Come on now, I am getting smarter and a lot tougher. I will now put these men through the grill. Guys, I feel bad because I know there are real men on the internet, but I have to prove to myself that you are the real ones and not the Scammers and fakes that I have already spoken to. And if you say you're from the UK or working in Nigeria, man, I am really going to try to find out more if interested, or I might just tell you to take a hike.

I just turned in a man that tried to convince me he was the One. Then he was going to send me money to help me with my Ministry, saying it was a donation, then asked me to keep part of it and send him the biggest chunk of it. And then had the gall to get mad at me when I told him that I would not do it and for him to keep his money. I told him I didn't want any part of it. Silly man, he had someone send me the checks anyway. It was supposed to be a small amount, not two checks. Then he told me again to deposit them and keep some of it and send him the biggest part of it. I don't know if he was bold or just plain Stupid. I told him that part of what I did on the internet was check people for scamming to help my Singles' group on Facebook: Sunwhisp's Christian's Singles Corner!

The thing was I told this man I was not interested in him, because we were going in different directions in what we wanted out of life. I am Ministry minded, and he wanted someone to be a Mother to his children. But he said he would be happy to just be friends. Another lesson learned. Just let them go and don't talk to them anymore. If all they can talk about is how much they want you to be their wife, and they barely talked to you get a clue.

Well, anyway, I write about my own experiences, because hopefully it will help someone else not fall into the trap these men set for women. I know there are women on the net that are doing this also. Some are really not women at all; they are men using woman's photos to get these men to send them money. Usually, wanting you to wire the money, like this scammer tried to get me to do.

So, men, don't get defensive if I ask you a lot of questions and ask you for some real photos. I have to protect myself, and I don't want any more Scammers in my life. Beware, I will turn you in. I am getting pretty savvy in detecting who you are, and the Banks are very appreciative to catch you. And the women you think are just lonely and vulnerable because they are single may be your worst nightmare. And remember, Christian Women have a pretty big God that will squish you like a bug if you mess with His Children. We are daughters of the King. We are the King's Kids. Woo-Hoo!

So the next time you meet someone on the Net and you find them appealing, check them out. Know who you are talking to. Don't feel bad if you ask them lots of questions. Google them and do a little background checking. That goes for the men too. If they are not willing to give you the information you need, just keep moving. God has that special person for you. I am still hoping mine is coming to me, and not on the net, but my God can bring him any way He wants to because He is God.

Blessings and Hugs,
Margene/Sunwhisp ❤ ❤ ❤

www.mywebface.com

Heartbreak-Detective Coolhand and Sunwhisp

My Heart was to do Ministry, so I found
Paltalk on the Internet. I sought out different
Christian groups. It was exciting to find a place on
the Internet that you could be with a group of people that could actually hear you. It was also wonderful to be a leader and be able to speak into other
people's lives. The best part was to hear from others
that they could feel the Holy Spirit when I spoke or
prayed for others. This was the early years in 2000.

I got to meet a lot of people through Paltalk. I also enjoyed getting to know men through Paltalk. I got to meet a few people in person.

The night I met Detective Coolhand changed my life. He came into the Room, and I heard his voice and my heart melted. I asked the owner of the Room who he was, and he said he would introduce us. "Detective Coolhand, this is Sunwhisp."

That opened the door to a Romance on Paltalk. What happened to all the other men that were interested in me? My heart was closed to them. I hate to say this, but women are earphoent and love to hear what a man has to say about us. I was a goner.

I kept talking to him about doing Ministry with me.

I continued leading the Rooms and meeting other people online.

I was getting distracted. I still loved Jesus with all my Heart. People knew about Detective Coolhand and me. There were other romances going on. People even talking about getting Married.

Then it happened, 9/11. He came to tell me that he was going to Afghanistan. The deception began. He told me he went to Afghanistan, and I didn't think I would ever hear from him again, and then he contacted me. How could that be? I didn't think they would allow him to call me or be on the internet. But lo and behold, there he was talking to me and not missing a beat. But some-

thing changed in me. I was no longer that confident person that he had first met on Paltalk. I was so concerned about him. He would contact me and tell me about accidents he had on Helicopters. And it was so real to me because later on the news, I would hear about a Helicopter going down. How the wind had caused the Helicopter to crash.

One day he called me and then asked if it was okay to talk on a three-way call with another woman. I said okay, and we talked, and then he said he needed to just talk to this woman because she was going through a rough time. He said he would call me back, and I felt really weird about that, but he hung up and talked to her. He called me back and said that he felt really bad, because he fell in love with two women. I told him that he would have to choose. He told me that he chose her. My heart was broken. Then I remembered a warning dream I had just the night before. It was about a woman trying to steal my man. But now I know another woman can't steal a man that she never had. I thought I was going crazy. How could I feel like I loved this man that I never met, and to be honest with you, I would not even give this guy a second look if I would meet him on the Street. He was skinny, and not even good looking. The only thing he had was a line of bull.

Scammers, Counterfeits, Fakes!

My Sister had originally opened the Door for me after my Divorce, and she said I could come and stay with her, and then I moved to St. Petersburg and lived with my niece, and then I moved into an Apartment by myself and was working for Temp Agencies and doing my Ministry on Paltalk, where many said they could feel the Presence of the HOLY SPIRIT when I led the Room, Praying for HEALING, etc. That is where the story of how I got so messed up came about. (The enemy used a man to try to destroy me.) Thinking, how could a Woman of God get so torn apart? Then I looked in the Bible of all the people that came into Depression. My Sister again opened the Door for me to come back and stay with her till my heart was healed.

I prayed and asked God to protect me from Counterfeits. So for years, I stayed off of the Internet and felt like no guy was looking at me. When I went back on the Internet and joined Facebook, the enemy tried it again. Detective Coolhand never asked me for money, but this man eventually did.

Jack was on Facebook. This good-looking guy asked me to be his friend on Facebook. He then proceeded to send me a letter that said he was going to Inherit a lot of money. He had an Attorney that verified to me that what he said was true. Jack told me he worked for a Business that helped Children. On and on his story went. His story was not the classic Scammer story. He was not an Engineer, and he did not have a wife that died, and he didn't have any children.

My Sister and niece had to prove to me that he was a Scammer. Again, I was on this wild trip, but in the back of my mind, I knew the truth. So I was checking him out. He said he was from England, but for business, he needed to go to Nigeria. And then kept telling me he was trying to leave Nigeria. There was another older married woman that thought he was real because of the things he said to me. He would write on my page how much he loved me, etc. Then My sister and niece did not believe that I knew how to take care of myself. Then he told me that he was going to come see me but needed some money to come. He had never asked me for any money before. I told him that I could not help him, and that if he really loved me, he would find a way. I told this woman not to give him any money, if he asked her. But she sent him some money, and then said he did not get it in time and that the Airline was going to charge him more. I told him I was not going to send him any. She got mad at me, because even though he told her that he would pay her back, he never did. I never heard from Jack again. I did contact his so-called Lawyer, and he told me just to forget about Jack. Therefore, what do you think? Was he a Scammer or not? I told my sister that there had to be a man behind the picture. Meaning the Scammers stole this man's pictures and used it to try to Scam women. Romance Scammers are horrible.

Women and men, stop being so desperate for love. You are better than that. I have been approached by many Scammers, and so I developed a Scammer page named Sunwhisp's Scammer Patrol!

God Bringing Me to Suncoast Worship Center!

My heart was broken when I came back to Englewood, Florida, and I didn't know if it would ever mend, But GOD! My Sister told me she was going to take over my LIFE, and I was needing her to do that. That is how hurt and messed up I was. (You can read my story of the reason why.) I enrolled in classes at MCC Manatee Community College, where I worked at the Career Center with a wonderful Woman named Wanda Kenney, who let and helped me heal by just listening to me, and she recommended a Church near where my Sister lived. There I met a wonderful Woman named Belinda that told me about a Woman's Group that met on Thursday Nights. She told me the Women will help me heal and speak into my life. That is where I met Deena, Valora, and several other women that loved me into recovery. Deena laughed at me because God was showing her I thought I was too old to go into Ministry. They Prophesied, held me when I cried, told me the

Father was giving me the name HOPE, because I would give others HOPE because of what I went through. They showed me the LOVE OF JESUS in everything they said and done for me. To this day, I have not forgotten them. And continue to LOVE them. I will never be able to Thank them enough for allowing the HOLY SPIRIT to use them in my Healing of my HEART.

As things progressed for the Healing of my Heart, I was led to the Women's Resource Center in Venice, Florida, and they listened to my Story, and even though it sounded so farfetched, they listened in LOVE, and they encouraged me that I could do what I needed to do.

Before going to the Church with Belinda, Deena, and Valora. I went to a small Church where I met Brian, and his wife, and he listened to me and encouraged me and told me that God was healing me.

One thing I noticed even in myself, that when I looked in the MIRROR, I did not recognize myself. It was almost like I was just looking at a shell of a body and the person that I was, was not there. You know, like the movies with the Zombies.

My eyes were like a blank canvas, empty and void.

But my healing was in process. One thing that Deena and Valora told me is that God was always with me. The things that I thought the enemy was doing was God getting me out of the situation, because *HE* was not going to allow the enemy to continue to toy with my mind.

Through that Ministry came the most healing, because it was one on one contact, and I could help other women with my Story.

One thing I kept asking God is how could something like this happen to me, someone that believed in *HIM* with all her Heart and be so devoted in following *HIM*. And He prompted me to look in the Bible at all the Stories of *HIS* great women and men that succumbed to Depression and Anxiety.

David even had to encourage himself. Elijah hid in a cave because Jezebel threatened him. And he just slayed thousands of her Prophets.

One of my favorite Gifts is *PROPHESY!*

I remember one time while going to Suncoast Worship Center. I was whining to God—yes, I said whining. Telling *HIM* how disappointed I was that the Pastor was spending time with *EVERYONE ELSE* but hardly a word to me, and no Prophecy, and then he just passed me by. I was about to cry. I felt so hurt. But my Abba Father asked me, "Why do you want so badly to hear a word from me through a mere man when I just gave you a word this morning? Can I not speak to you *MYSELF?*" I felt so humbled and realized my foolish whining. When *HE* wants to speak to you, *HE* doesn't always speak through someone else. When *HE* speaks through someone else, it usually to confirm what *HE* has already been speaking to you.

I have to admit I still love getting a word from GOD through others, but I love it when HE tells me HIMSELF. Wonderful, I love those times. I also love giving others a Word that HE gives me for them. Learning of HOW MUCH HE LOVES me. PRICELESS.

Quiet yourself and listen. HE is waiting to talk to you. Enjoy HIS loving PRESENCE. Better than Silver and Gold, and Diamonds don't sparkle as much as HIS loving words for what HE has for you alone. May this bless you.

Love,

Margene Wiese-Baier 2017

Ministry at Suncoast

I began to be able to work in the different Ministries at Suncoast. I wanted to be in Choir, but because of my School Schedule and working part time, I was too exhausted to do anything else. Even though I was in Church every minute I could be. At that time, we were still in the little Church, and that is where I first heard Bill Cameron, and he was telling us about the Ministry that God gave him: TEAM JESUS 2000. When I heard all of the details, I said to myself, "That is what I want to do."

Bill and his wife, Charlene, went to areas in Florida and distributed food, clothing, and a hot meal to the homeless and migrant workers and people in need, but it didn't stop in Florida.

They went throughout the United States, Haiti, Honduras, etc., and Bill also Ministered at a local Nursing Home. That was the day I fell in love with MISSIONS.

I went to Honduras on a Mission trip that was under the Ministry of the Church, which is now LIFEGIVERS...Pastors Tom and Brenda Jones. Charlene Cameron and Bill Schmidt were both on that trip and watched over me.

On that trip, I was also there with a woman that became my best friend, Liz. On that trip, several people got Pink eye, which was running rapid. We went to one Church and were being Prophesied over, and one of the Women said to continue to LOVE people, and my well would never run dry; the more I give out, the more will be poured into me. The HOLY SPIRIT taught me before I even left the HUG MINISTRY, and I would be the arms around them, but it was the Father's love that would pour into them. On that trip, we went to mountains where the garbage was being burned. The Children would come around me and cuddle with me, and even though the bugs would be crawling, it did not matter. I was protected with HIS love, and HE wanted to embrace them by using me. What an HONOR! In other places where women were hurting so bad because of abuse, HIS LOVE SHOWED UP, and I was to embrace two women at a time, and the older one was to become the younger one's mentor, like a Mother. On and on God was showing HIS FATHERLY LOVE for

THEM, and to me too. These are only a very min-ute amount of Stories that unfolded on that trip.

The last Mission trip I went on with a School that was started at that Church was a Medical Mission Trip, but Pastor Brenda used wisdom and listened to the HOLY SPIRIT and allowed me to Pray for people. I was part of a Prayer group with Susan White and another woman. The funny thing is they let me do all of the praying. I sat in a chair in the midst of all these beautiful people that had seen the Doctors first, and then they would come to me, and I would pray over them. Two Honduran women were assigned to me. I prayed and asked God that they would understand every-thing I said to them. I prayed for many people on that particular day, but two Miracles stand out in my Memory. The first one was a little boy that looked like he was going to die. Susan White brought him to me and put him in my arms. He was so limp and lifeless. All I knew to do was to sing in the Spirit and hold him close to me so he wouldn't fall. A Momma Seta danced and prayed before me. I do not know how long this went on, but it felt like hours. Now remember, there are many waiting to be prayed for. Finally, I opened my eyes and saw the older woman in front of me, and the little boy's eyes were barely open, and I said to him, "Loco Inspirito," and he said, "Loco." It was like at that moment, he was instantly healed. Susan White came over to me and told me that she was going to take him back to show the Doctors, and then she brought him back and said she was going to give him some bread. Local bakeries donated fresh bread for the people to eat while they were waiting. Glory to God the Father. That little boy was totally healed. I was praying for another person and looked up and saw the little boy devouring the Bread. The BREAD of LIFE. Hallelujah!

Then I saw before me a Mother and daughter with a weird red coloring on their faces. I knew that it was not a Sunburn, so I told the Lord, "Something looks very wrong with these women." He revealed to me that they were processed by an evil spirit. (Many people in Honduras went to Witch Doctors and are very used to the Spiritual Realm, so that is why when Jesus is introduced to them. They will accept HIM Because HE is good.) Okay, on with the story. I looked at the woman and told my helpers not to touch her until whatever was in her left. Now remember, I had never dealt with this before (Okay, side story, before I left on this Mission trip, a woman told me in front of the Church while I was Worshiping and Praising that I would be doing the Deliverance Ministry. Come on now, I am into the love Ministry. I told God, "I don't know…I don't really want to do that"), but I was willing if that is what HE wanted me to do. The HOLY SPIRIT was so gentle with me. I was told before I left, I would not have to yell at these things to have them come out of people. Well, the woman started spitting up on the floor, and I started getting loud, and Susan White came up to me and told me, "Margene, you don't have to yell at it. It is already coming out of her." Susan said, "It is time to tell her to say the name Jesus."

I asked her about three times and then She said, "JESUS, JESUS, JESUS!" The redness in her face left, and a smile crossed her lips. She was a beautiful sight. Then I asked my helpers to pray with her, leading her the rest of the way in knowing Jesus as her Savior. I then prayed for her daughter. It didn't take as long with her, and again the redness was replaced with a smile. Her continence changed, and her skin changed from red to a natural color. Later I saw the woman still in a glowing smile. She told me, "So sorry for you," and I told her, "Oh no, it was a good thing," and that I was glad that God used me to help her. No one took pictures of either the little boy or the woman and her daughter to my knowledge, but there were many witnesses that can tell you this is all true. Showing if you allow the Holy Spirit to work through you, Miracles can and will happen.

Okay, that is just part of the things that have occurred in my LIFE to share with you, and I will share more later. But just remember, we are the Church, we are the LOVE, and HE will work through each one of us if we open up our HEARTS to HIM. That is why I will shout it from the rooftops that I am a lover of JESUS CHRIST. I am a BELIEVER, and I want HIM TO WORK

THROUGH ME to LOVE Everyone that HE PUTS IN MY PATH.

I LOVE YOU, LORD, I will lift my Voice: http://www.youtube.com/watch?v=C6WexG9uAJI

New International Version (©1984)
>	For God did not send his Son into the world to condemn the world, but to save the world through Him.

New Living Translation (©2007)
>	God sent his Son into the world not to judge the world, but to save the world through Him.

English Standard Version (©2001)
>	For God did not send his Son into the world to condemn the world, but in order that the world might be saved through Him.

New American Standard Bible (©1995)
>	For God did not send the Son into the world to judge the world, but that the world might be saved through Him.

King James Bible (Cambridge Ed.)
>	For God sent not his Son into the world to condemn the world; but that the world through him might be saved.

http://bible.cc/john/3-17.htm

How Do you See Me Inside Out?
HE sees me as Beautiful!

He is Here! Photo taken by
Margene Wiese-Baier © 2012

Honduras Mission Trip

If you can go to my YouTube and watch, then it will keep count of how many viewed them,

And you can also see the other videos I made, including the ones I made of Kobie and the local Churches in the Area.
February 4, 2012, at 11:13 a.m.

A friend wrote,
> Every time I think of you, I give thanks to my God. I always pray for you, and I make my requests with a heart full of joy because you have been my partner in spreading the Good News about Christ from the time we first became friends. And I am sure that God, who began the good work within us, will continue his work until it is finally finished on that day when Christ Jesus comes back for us. Philippians 1:3-6

Singles Ministry

One day I went to see Pastor Phillip and asked him what was going to happen with the Singles Group. And lo and behold, I was the only one that asked about it, so he asked me to be the head of the Group. I told him that I would do it until someone else wanted to do it. Well, he also asked a man that went to Church to be my Co-Leader. I had all sorts of plans. The Pastor allowed me to have an introductory lunch, and there was a lot of interest. Men and Women came, and we had a great time.

I made a list of things that I wanted to happen. We joined together with another Singles Group in Florida, and it was fun having them visit. We got together, and Pastor Phillip came, and I got to sing with him. That was such a highlight in my life. We had so much fun, and I believe everyone that came enjoyed the night too.

Before my Singles Group started and the other group still existed, I had met this man, and we seemed to hit it off, but God said no. It was an Audible no. I would go to the Cameron's Home Group, and this man would sit by me, and every time I would move, he would move by me. How crazy. I had waited for someone to be interested in me, and here was a handsome Christian man that was pursuing me. I remember going to a luncheon after Church, and he was talking about a past relationship, and it stood out to me when he said, that she took him away from Church and they lived together. That made me realize that the same thing could happen if I let it. But I was not going to let that happen.

He continued to pursue me. I even had a friend tell me to give him a chance, but the no from God kept ringing in my ears. This man and I were a great team doing Ministry. I would pray for the people at Church, and he was my Catcher. One time I went with Brian Hagerty's men's group to a Church and helped them do Ministry. It was so much fun. Brian wanted me to go to pray for the women at the Church. Again, I had my partner, my catcher, with me. I kept wondering why God was saying no to me. But it was still a No.

So my Singles group began, and it was off to a good start.

Then it happened. My co-leader came aboard, and it was downhill from then on. There really was not many rules, but that if a woman needed help, she was supposed to come to me, and the men go to him. I talked to the Pastor about this, and he told me not to worry about it, that I could send the men to him. I had so many plans, but my co-leader did not want to do anything but just meet at the Church. The room was dark and so uninviting. It was the Teen Room, and they painted the room black. Slowly the members dropped off till it was only women coming. It was depressing to me, and I was soon losing interest in being a Leader and turned it over to the Man. He didn't really have time to run it. So again the Singles Group disappeared.

Nothing ever happened with the man that God said No about. And then he left the Church. I saw him years ago just before I went to India. We were so excited to see each other. This was at another Church in Englewood just around the corner from Suncoast. When I got back from India, I went to see if he was still going there and see if the answer was still no. He was there, and we sat by each other. He began telling me about a woman he was seeing and how she wanted to Marry him, but he was not sure. I do not know why he told me all of that, but I knew that God's answer was still NO!

Answered Prayer for Marriage for a Friend

I was talking to a friend earlier today, and I remembered a friend that I worked with, and she was crying to me that she didn't think she would ever meet anyone. She was lonely after her husband that she loved passed away. It had been five years at that time. I said to her, "Okay...We are going to pray about this right now, in the store." God set it up because we didn't have any customers in the Store. I said a passionate prayer over her at the Holy Spirit's leading, and within a week, a man that she is now married to moved in a home right behind her. Whoop! Whoop! Another time a young man that seemed to be a leader in the young group. Well, anywho, I was talking to Him, and I was led to tell him. He was the most mature one in the group, and he was ready to get married. Not long after that, God revealed to him his wife, someone he already knew but didn't see her in that way until then. I didn't know that you were not supposed to tell people these type of things. All I know is when God shows you something beautiful, you need to take the chance and tell them. The thing is when you prophesy over someone, you don't know when it is going to happen, because it is in HIS timing but to tell someone after the fact is not so believable. Our FATHER wants us to share love with each other. What better way than to pray the love of their life into it. GOD is LOVE, and LOVE is GOD

The Honduran girl I met.
Pastel I did while I was going to MCC.
I used this for my teacher's class.

Honduran Pastor and an older
Honduran woman

How Do you See Me Inside Out?
HE sees me as Beautiful!

Honduran Moms and their Children waiting
to see the Doctors on a Medical Mission Trip.

Honduras Mission Trip in 2005!

Helping a Friend with Her Parents

When the Owners of the Duplex I lived at in Englewood sold it, I needed to move. I moved in with a friend and her husband.

One of my friends asked me to go with her on a trip to help her put her parents in Nursing Homes. It was a wild trip. Her parents were both sick. Her mom had been sick for years, and her dad was her caregiver but was getting tired, and he needed a break. So out of respect, I will deduce that they both needed to be in Nursing homes to get the help they needed. So we got busy and located a home for both of us. While her mom was put in the Hospital to help this project along, we got to stay at a House designated to help families with family members staying at the Hospital.

While on this adventure, the enemy was on the attack for both of us. This was the reason my friend asked me to go with her, because she knew I knew how to pray.

The women at the House we stayed at were wonderful. Even though it was not the most fun reason to be on an Adventure, but they made it more bearable.

So we accomplished getting both of her parents in Nursing homes, so we we're going home.

Living in Port Charlotte

Living in Port Charlotte was special, because it was the City where my parents lived for a while. My Mom had passed during the time they lived there. Actually, when I moved to Florida, I thought I would want to move to Punta Gorda. That is where my Sister worked as an Editor for the newspaper. Punta Gorda was a beautiful quaint place that had lots of events that Movies are made of, or Hallmark Moments. It was a wealthy place, and when I first moved to Florida, I was told that I could live anywhere. My credit score was that good, but how could I get a place when I did not even have a job? But even at that, I still wanted to look. The problem was that the Real Estate people were just showing me homes in Port Charlotte.

Then Hurricane Charlie hit while I lived in Englewood, and even though Englewood was spared, Punta Gorda was practically destroyed and had to be rebuilt.

So years later, I was moving into an Apartment in Port Charlotte. They let me pick out colors of paint for a wall in my living room to be painted. I picked pink, and they allowed it. The original colors of choice were bland and boring. But the pink was beautiful. And the Berber carpet was easy to keep clean and much softer than what I remembered. So here I was in the office talking to the woman I first rented the

Apartment from in Port Charlotte. I had bandages on my face and a sling on my arm. I was quite a sight. Thankfully, because I did not have any money, I was able to get help from different organizations to pay my rent. In fact, it was the Catholic Church that helped me the most. I had gone in there and was sitting, waiting. Then I was called in to an office and was asked a lot of questions. The ordinary process is to go to several Places and get a portion of the money and added together, would pay the rent. I told the man that I didn't know if I could do that because of being so hurt. He told me to wait a few minutes, and when he came back, he told me they were going to take care of it. I was elated to hear that. That was so nice, and I thank Abba Father for such a blessing. I not only found favor with them but was helped by other organizations. My friend was my human Angel and took good care of me. I stayed with her because I could not be by myself, and it was easier to stay with her than for her to come to my Apartment. I stayed with her for a few weeks and then was able to go home.

Thankfully, I was able to get Unemployment and had to look for a job. With no luck. So I had to look for something that I could afford. Because of my broken shoulder that was not healing very fast, and I still could not drive. It was getting harder to pay the rent, so I knew I needed to move to a place that I could afford. My Lease was up, so it was a perfect time to move. That is when I went to see about getting into Rotonda Lakes Apartments. Hallelujah!

Moving to Rotonda, Florida

The Loneliness did not go away by moving into a beautiful new apartment.

My sister went with me to check out the Apartment at Rotonda Apartments. She told me it was a no-brainer to move into the Apartment because it was such a good deal. They had a special deal going on, and I could get in at a reduced amount. Normal rent was outrageous, and I would not be able to pay that amount. I was having a hard time because the Apartments was out in the Boondocks and I did not have a car, because I hadn't driven since I got hurt in March of 2009. So you see, I did not see it as a no-brainer but a sentence of being all alone, but I moved in, nonetheless. And my Adventure there began. I was thinking I made a mistake, because in the building across from me, a woman died in one of the Apartments. It freaked me out. I was ready to find a different place. The woman had been dead for over a month, and no one knew it, but people started complaining about the smell. Unbelievable, she had a little dog that was eating her to stay alive. That was creepy. I do not know what they did with the dog. It really was not the dog's fault that he or she had to do that. How could someone be dead for a month and no one checked on her? She even had a Mother that lived at the complex also. What about the people that worked there? She owed rent, and no one tried to go collect it from her. But here I was living in a beautiful Apartment. My best friend later moved in to her own apartment. That eased the pain of not having a vehicle to get around. She was my saving Grace, and we were together almost every day. I was thankful, since she was the friend that I had that I fell on the sidewalk where she lived. She had taken care of me after I got out of the Hospital. She had been told some lies, and she stopped talking to me for a while. Then one day she came to see someone at the Apartments, and I saw her and stopped her, and we got to talk and I got to give my side of the story. It is amazing how people can cause such destruction in relationships by lying. I was so glad to have her as a friend again.

We went to several different Churches together while at both the Apartments in Port Charlotte and in Rotonda. We went to one little Church where they sang songs that were like Country music. We went on Friday nights because we wanted something to do. It was fun, and at one of the services, the Pastor said, "I feel the Lord wants us to give you a hundred dollars to pay for a bill." He had his wife get out their checkbook and she made out a check. That is the first time that ever happened. Later when I moved to Rotonda, they got some men together and helped me move.

Sometimes it is confusing to me because the Apartments I lived at looked so much alike.

Prophet or a Mere Man

I remember when I first saw him on Facebook, I thought he was so handsome. He had a crazy little smile that caught my eye. I don't even like beards or messy hair on a guy, but there was something about him that told me to give him a second look. He was doing a Ministry on Facebook, and yes, I saw that he was followed mainly by women, but I did not let that hinder me from talking to him. For some reason, I knew that we would become friends, if nothing more. At that time, I was looking for someone I could do Ministry with. I had my goals of what I thought my Destiny was, and I thought this man was going to help me fulfill them. So this saga of my life began. I did not know at the time how everything would turn out, but when he asked if we could meet, I asked my best friend at that time if she would come with me. So off we went to meet him and one of his Ministry friends at a Restaurant. I saw that he looked like his pictures, and that pleased me. He was a little stockier, but still just as handsome. I sat by him. I have a habit of touching people on their arm, and he did not pull away from me, and that was a plus. The meeting went well as he told me about the Ministry that he wanted to get started on ending the Sex Trafficking in

Florida. He really didn't seem to be interested in the Ministry that I wanted to do. I listened, and I remembered the Prophesy over me that I would be working with Prostitutes and bringing them out of Bondage. His friend was super nice. But did not talk a whole lot but told about his family and how much he loved them. Then we went to his home. I felt safe, because my friend was with me. We continued to talk about Ministry. Then we went home. I kept in contact with this man, and later we talked about him coming to where I lived. I told him if he was interested in someone else that he should not come. He asked me why, and I told him, because if he was interested in someone else, then he would probably want to do Ministry with that person. I started having financial problems, and I told him, and he decided to go stay at another woman's home. He was supposed to be staying at a house that had been her parents'. When he got there, he found out that the house was not ready to have anyone live in it, so he ended up living with her. She had in mind that he would fall in love with her. He had no intentions of that and just wanted a place to hold over till he came to be with me. After he left her house, her house ended up burning down. I let him come not knowing what had happened at the woman's house. Again, I told him that if he was interested in another woman, not to come. I don't know why I kept thinking it was okay to let him come. I really wanted a Partner in Ministry. He kept talking to me about how the Widow woman provided for Elijah. Again, I was duped. How could I have been so deceived. In my heart, I was really hoping and praying that this was the Man God sent to me. Not only for Ministry, but my Partner in life. He came, and from the beginning, I could see that this was not the case. He was on the phone immediately with his old girlfriend. He would talk to her right in front of me. They would always end their conversation with telling each other that they loved each other. I felt betrayed from the start because I had asked him not to come if he was interested in someone else. Later he told me that he used his ex-girlfriend on this other woman, so she would not get interested in him. Could he be giving me a little hint in what he was doing with me? A few days later, we went to see a Hotel that a Church invited me to go see and go out to Lunch. I took him with me. While there, he decided to go walking on the Beach. He did not even walk on the tour to look at the Hotel. It was about time to leave, so some of the people helped me go look for him. We found him, and we started walking back to the Restaurant, and I fell in the sand. And I struggled and struggled to get up in the sinking sand. He did not even try to help me up, but just looked at me while I struggled. At that moment, I knew the truth—that he was not the man I had been praying for. But I let him stay. We were supposed to do things together, but he went places of Ministry by himself. And came back early on sick, and I caught whatever he had. How could I just kick him out then? I know I was sure not very attractive being so sick. His ex-girlfriend told him to go swim in the Ocean. It was so cold outside. I was so angry with her that she would tell him that because I knew it would just make him sicker. Even though I was sick too, I had been making soup, trying to get us well. We were becoming good friends, but I was beginning to know that we would not become anything more. I was not interested in making myself attractive to him. I was thankful that he had his own room and bathroom.

I took him to some of the Churches, and he would barely even sit by me saying that his back hurt him. I would try to introduce him to the Pastors, and he would introduce himself. What the Hey! That was not the plan. We were supposed to be working together.

It sure wasn't going the way I had envisioned. I thought I was hearing from God in letting him come. I was giving up more and more of my Dreams to help this man fulfill his. The red flags were coming up more and more. His so-called ex- girlfriend told him that we all needed to or separate things and then come together. What? That was not what was supposed to happen. He told me not to work with this one young woman, because his girlfriend was more equipped to help her. What? I kept thinking back to the Prophesy of working with women that had sexual problems.

Then we went to the Church I had been going to and actually had worked with for a while. I got to sing with the Pastor and treasured that time. I could not believe what happened. We walked through the door, and women acted like a pack in heat. Come on now, I was the one with him, but he acted like he did not even know me. He walked around, and then the Pastor asked if anyone had anything, and I spoke up, and then this man spoke up. His word was not accepted very well. Then he went to this one woman, and whatever he told her upset her, and she told the Pastor. He also told a woman's husband that his wife should not sing. Who was this man I thought I could trust? Who did I allow in my home? Well, he was not like this in my home. This man that I was introducing to people was not the same man. Later I was called and was told that I needed to talk to him. I did, but he did not receive it very well and said that they should be the ones to tell him. That is what I felt too, and the Pastor and him were supposed to have lunch, but it never happened. Only a phone call.

"Abba Father," I was praying, "I do not believe that we were meant to do Ministry together. I need you to get him out of my Apartment." He had brought his dog there, and that was the answer. My Apartment Manager came to the door the next day and told me that the dog was not permitted to be at the Apartment complex, because they were known to be dogs that could turn violent, and they could not take the chance of him hurting anyone. I had a week to get him off the Property. This man heard me talking to her and came and talked to her and told her that the dog was not a full-blooded breed. But she did not care and told him that he had to go. Thankful, that is what I needed to make him leave. So funny she did not say he had to leave, but so be it. God used his dog to make him move. For someone that acted like he had nowhere to go, he left in a couple days and didn't take all the time she gave him. Amazing, God, YOU protected me again. There is so much more to this story, but I am not out to take revenge on anyone, but to show that if we do not watch it, that we can create our own problems. I am most thankful that I did not sleep with this man. We became friends, and I was told many times that he was just using me, but I wanted Love and a Ministry so much that I got twisted up in a tangled web that could have destroyed me. After he left, I had a friend Tena take some pictures of me, and he asked if I was trying to be a Deva. You see, he tried taking pictures of me, and they turned out disgusting. God did not allow me to be Attractive while he was there to protect me. I did not find him attractive anymore almost from the beginning. I am thankful to my friends that did not abandon me, even though they were probably thinking I was sleeping with him. I assure you that I was not and again was saved by HIS Grace, In Jesus's Name. I am Thankful that even though he was angry with me and would not allow me to say anything in my defense. On the way out, all he could say is, "I pray you get closer to Jesus."

Remember the woman that he did not want me to talk to anymore? She was supposed to have a transplant. She ended up dying before she could have the transplant. The Doctors kept telling her she was not bad enough yet. How sad. She was very sweet. She apologized to me for telling the man things that were only supposed to be between the two of us. I think of her occasionally and know that she is Heaven now. I am thankful that I did not stop talking to her. I tried to encourage her about Jesus. Thankful.

An Indian Pastor! The Dream... from Heaven or Hell!

After I went to India, I thought maybe I was to Marry an Indian man. While over there, they seemed to find me very Attractive. They made me feel like a Movie Star. Because I had Blonde hair and fair skin, they seemed intrigued by me. They would stare at me. I found many of them very attractive.

One time a whole group of them on Motorcycles stopped and looked at me. I waved at them like I was Marilyn Monroe. This was so good for my Morale. After years of feeling like no men noticed me, to be somewhere where many seemed to notice me. It was a totally different World over in India.

Similar to Honduras, but not the same reaction even though the men in Honduras found me intriguing, they did not seem to look at me in the same way. In Honduras, I was with a Ministry Team, and maybe that was the difference, and in India I was with my friends, a Married Couple that did Ministry. We went somewhere almost every day that exposed me to many people. Seeing the devastation of Poverty everywhere. I saw the similarities of Honduras and India, but I saw the difference between the people. It was almost like the People in Honduras were happier even though they were so poor. I got to know the Hondurans in a different way. Some of them confiding that they were Sexually Molested by their own Fathers from a young age. And the Fathers thinking they had that right. How sad. I know the same thing was happening in India! I know it happens here in America, but not tolerated like it is in these Countries. I am so disgusted with some of the horrible stories I hear about sex trafficking Worldwide. But what is even more is when a girl's own family gives their children over to be used by disgusting men.

One man contacted me that had a different look about him than the rest of the Indians. I found him very Attractive. He did not tell me until later that he was Married. I had a dream about him. Thinking it was from God, I contacted him and told him about the Dream. At the end of the Dream, we kissed. It was so real that I actually felt it. Not being kissed for a very long time, it was very special. This Dream was about a Man that lives in India that is also a friend here on Facebook.

I was dreaming that his People were building him a large house. There were many people working on it. I was there, and before I woke up, I walked up to him and I asked him if we could talk. The house was very large, and it seemed a part of it was already finished, and an L-shaped part was being built to connect with it (possibly the house he already has), So that would make it a large Rectangle building. When I woke up, I thought maybe it was really a Church being built. (This man is a Pastor.)

I contacted him after having the Dream, and we started talking again. Thinking this was a dream from God. Was I tricked again by the devil? He is truly out to Kill, Steal, and Destroy in my life. Then out of the blue, he was going to come to America to go to a Christian School that was helping people from other Countries set up Ministries in their Countries. How could this happen if not from God? The devil does not want God's work to be done. This man and I talked about getting together. He was staying with a Couple that he had met when they came to India. The man that he was staying with even talked to me about how honest this man from India was and how he had never asked for anything, but why were they asking me for money now? He was asking me to help his sons that were back home in India, telling me that he wanted me to come back with him. I thought it very strange, yet I was entranced with him. He would tell me how sexually attracted he was to me. I was very attracted to him, but yet very cautious. We had talked about meeting at a friend's Farm. I was not quite trusting him 'cause of what the other man had done with choosing the other woman over me. This woman was involved with someone else and told me she had no interest in him, but...but...but... that fear did hit me, I had to admit. I even told him that if GOD did not want him to come, that he would not come. He did not believe me, but I kept asking God to protect me if he was not the one HE chose for me. And he was Married. Even though he kept telling me they were separated. He said he did not Divorce her because he did not want to hurt his Church. This did not make sense to me that he could still Preach and God use him if he was not being faithful to his wife. But I would keep thinking the rules were different there in India. But deep in my Heart, the rules for God were Worldwide. I can see now how the enemy was out to deceive me. And even my friend was being deceived.

Oh, back to his friend talking to me about helping him financially. I did send him a small amount of money. He asked me for more, and I did not send him more, and he got angry. I was not making very much, and I had told him that. He later apologized to me. The truth of the matter was, he was another user. When it came right down to it. God was not going to allow him to come. The red flags and roadblocks were right there, and finally God sent him back to India. Yes, he was very handsome and charming, but he was not the Man Abba Father had for me. So I am thankful I never met him Personally. It would have been a Blunder. To this day, my friend and I talk about it. How could he have fooled both of us? And what would have happened if he would have come on that Farm? He has tried to contact me since then, and her too. He has been blocked. I hope this shows other women to be very careful in allowing men to fool them. Not to be needy. Remember, God will protect. Ask...HE will honor you.

Life goes on. It is Amazing that when things happen to us, that with HIS help, we can make it through them. Thinking that someone is meant for you and then HE shows you that if you would be with them, your Life would not be what HE has planned for you. Like if I would have gone to India to be with that Pastor, I would be living in Poverty and would be a woman in hiding, because how could I be in Public with a man that was Married to someone else? Besides, how do I know what he was telling me was the truth? I knew he was in Ministry because I saw the pictures, but the other things about his wife, Truth or Lies. She was probably very beautiful. So the ending of another saga to my Life. I was lonely but Thankful, that I knew that I was honoring my *Abba Father* by not pushing my will. Allowing *Him* to show me and listening was the *Key* to my *Future*.

Medical Records and Memories

A few years ago, I needed to get my *Medical Records* to provide evidence that I was telling the truth about my conditions to get *Money* to live on. I contacted the *Clinic* I had gone to and was able to get them. The woman that I contacted made copies and sent them to me. I was going through the *Records* and came across the *Records* of when I was having my first baby. I didn't realize how it was going to affect me. The tears that would come that were hidden for all those years. I did not know that the *Clinic* did more than what I was told at the time. The pain was as if it just happened. So here goes...

We hadn't been *Married* that long when I found out that I was *Pregnant*. *Excited*, but part of me was hoping to have more time to get to know my new husband more before having a *Family*. Our *Marriage* was off to a shaky start. It seemed that all we did was fight. I hated fighting, but he seemed to enjoy fighting. We fought before we got *Married*. At that time, I thought that things would change after we got *Married*. I don't know why. I was so *Naive*. I remember the day before we got *Married*, we were at his *Sister's* house, and he told me that maybe we should not get *Married*, because our kids would be teased, because they were part Japanese. I cried and cried. But maybe he was right. But I thought if we got Married, it was meant to be. Finding out that is a Stupid way to think. Never just let things happen. From Him saying what he did it was like he Prophesied how things would go in our Marriage. Sad but true, words are Powerful. So we were standing in front of the Pastor taking our vows. After walking in with my Dad, I wanted to run, but here I was standing there and just before the Pastor asked me if I accepted him as a husband, my husband to be said he saw the devil up in the corner of the Church. Later, actually many years after, he told me it was a Spider on a Spiderweb. But to me, it was like a curse over our Marriage. He had been drinking with the Pastor before the Wedding. So here we were, getting Married, and I was not sure at all that I was doing the right thing. But we both said "I do," And then off to our Honeymoon at the Coast. Cold and yucky, dark and gloomy. Staying in his little trailer. Rats coming in and out. So sick. What a way to start a Marriage. But we were Married now. Making the best of it. He was a good man, but finding that he really was not the one I should have Married. Getting Pregnant right away. Having to admit that I was probably pregnant before we got Married. He was the first man that I ever slept with. I had been keeping myself for the man I would marry. The months went by, and then we went on an outing, picking Mushrooms, but I felt so sick. I felt like I was dying, not knowing that my baby was dying inside of me. So when I got home, I called my Doctor. I loved my Doctor. He told me that I needed to come in and get checked. I was sitting in the waiting room, and I heard them talking about me, thinking I left. But I called out and said I did not leave. They checked me in and proceeded to take the biggest needle, and it was so long and took out some amniotic fluid out of my uterus. He told me that the baby had died and that I would have to go to the Hospital and the baby would have to come out so It would not poison me. I felt so guilty to even think I was the one dying. I thought I had walking Pneumonia. I don't know if I ever felt so sick.

So here I was lying in the Hospital bed and waiting for my baby to come out of me. Waiting for a baby that would come out, but not being alive. It was so sad. I didn't have anyone come to be with me except my husband. He tried his best. He was going through his own torment. I cried and cried. The doctor came in and found out the nurse had given me toilet paper and was upset with her because I could have gotten infection. Thankfully, I didn't and then I was asked to push, and she came out. I wanted to see her. I knew she would have dark hair and dark eyes. But the Doctor told me he did not want me to see her. He said he did not know why she died. I did not ask again, but regretted not looking at her.

So many questions would have been answered. The Doctor said they would take care of her. I didn't know what that meant. I asked him how far along I was, and he told me I was five or six months along. Why, oh why was this sweet little baby taken away from me? I named her after my brother, Daniel. I named her Danielle. After I got out of the Hospital, I later went in for a checkup. I went in the room and waited and waited and then the Nurse Practioner, MidWife finally came in, and the first thing she asked was why I had a D&C. I told her, "Because my baby died." She apologized all over herself. The thing is, if she would have read my Medical Records, she wouldn't have asked me such a hurtful question.

So, here years later, I went through these hurtful memories. Seeing that they looked over my little baby and even said that she looked like a Monster and it was a completely different description than what my Doctor gave me. He told me she was perfect. So who was telling the truth? Finding that my Husband felt guilty and thinking he was the cause, because he took lots of drugs while in Vietnam.

So here I was looking over the Medical Records several years later and wondering if her death had anything to do with Agent Orange. So I looked up what babies looked like, because of parents being exposed to Agent Orange. Being described as looking like Monsters. I went out to Oregon to talk to my ex and asked him questions at his house. He *was not very helpful. He said he did not remember anything from when our sweet baby died. So I was just spinning my wheels. I am thankful she was in Heaven and she does not look like a Monster. In my Heart I see her as a beautiful dark-haired girl. She went to Heaven, I am sure of that, because all babies go back to Heaven. Mom went to Heaven in 1985, and I know that they are there together with all my pets and her mom and dad and other relatives that have gone on before them and after. Though that was a painful day going through the Medical Records and also talking to my ex about Danielle, I know without a doubt where she is and that she did not have to grow up on Earth bearing the burden of not being born perfect. Also, easing the pain that others would inflict not only on her but me and my family.*

So, Beautiful Danielle, I look forward in seeing you and your Grandma someday. Love you forever, Mommy

The Wait is over! The Doctor said it was time to try again!

It was amazing that the Doctor said, "If you want, you can try again to get Pregnant."

Wow. That is all that I needed to hear. The next thing I knew I was being told, "You are going to have a baby." I was excited and looking forward to having another baby, only this time a baby that would grow up. So the day came, and my beautiful little girl was going to be born. My

Sister-in-Law had a Baby Shower while I was in the Hospital. Not very good timing. But I was becoming a Mommy. Her Daddy telling me to breathe and push...And here she came. My Mother-in-Law kept telling me she was going to look Japanese, but my whiteness was the dominant gene. So instead of dark silky hair and dark eyes, my little beauty had silky blonde hair and lighter eyes. The baby doctor told me how beautiful she was. I was so excited and felt like it was the happiest day of my life. I loved being pregnant, but I was even happier being a Mother. Her Daddy and I still didn't get along very well, but I wanted to be a family, so I put up with a lot.

Three years later, Another baby on her way!

I may not have been happy in my Marriage, but I loved being a Mommy. My little girl grew more beautiful every day and was super smart. She had good common sense for a three-year-old. I could not have loved a little girl more. I went to the Hospital to have her little sister. Well, this time my Mother-in-Law was right. I had a beautiful little dark haired, ebony-eyed baby girl. My neighbor brought her sister to look at her, and she was disappointed that she was not Black. I guess because I taught her to Love all colors, not just white children and Japanese. Unfortunately, no one gave her a Baby Shower. I guess because I was in the Hospital for my other daughter's shower, and my Sis-in-Law didn't want that to happen again. We were given things for her. And we felt so blessed having a Sweet new baby. Her sister soon fell in love with her baby sister and never said anything to me about being disappointed that she wasn't Black. I guess my neighbor thought it was cute that she said what she said. I had trouble nursing her, and when I went back into the Pediatrician's for a checkup, He told me that she was losing weight and asked me to show him how I was nursing her. He told me I had plenty of milk and then made sure she was latching on right. He then said it would be a shame to lose such a beautiful baby. To this day, I thought that it was unnecessary for him to make that remark. Not nice at all. From then on, she Flourished and gained weight. I was thankful I did not have any trouble getting her to nurse. The girls continued to grow to be best of friends. Her personality was completely different then her Sister's. She demanded Attention and would climb up into our laps if she needed hugs and cuddling, her sister seemed more independent. Even though Loving, she just wasn't as demanding. We would lie on the couch together and watch TV. My girls were my Life. Even though I did not have the ideal Marriage, I loved being a Mommy. I was not a very confident Mom, but I knew how much I loved my daughters. My girls were clingy when we went to Church. It was hard letting them go to Sunday School. I took them with me every Sunday. My Husband didn't go, saying his Church was out in Nature. I didn't know at the time but found out later that people thought I was a Single Parent. I also found out there was a lot of Gossip going on, especially this one little Church I went to for a while. A woman at the Church told me that the other women were talking about me, so he would come with me occasionally to eat at Potlucks. Church women are the best cooks...

High School Memories

I was talking to a new friend on Facebook who I went to High School with. And she told me some of the people she hung out with. I went to the same School almost my whole life, so I knew almost everyone. She moved there her Junior year. I got to thinking of the girls at School. I will not name any names because I do not want to embarrass anyone. They seem to be making movies of some of the things that happens in School. I am seeing that there is the Popular Group. In my School, I thought these were the nicest people in School. Then there were the meanies, the ones that picked on everyone. They were really the ones that did not feel good about themselves, so they picked on others to try to make themselves feel better. Then there was the quiet and shy group. Now I guess they would be called the Nerds, and Geeks. Yes, they were the ones that got the best grades. Most seemed to be shy but very Sweet. And then there were the ones that didn't really fit in any group. I didn't feel like I really belonged or fit in any group. I wanted to be in the Popular group but wanted to stand up for the shy, quiet ones. I wanted not to really follow anyone. I wanted to be me, and that sometimes left me feeling lonely, and I guess I still have that young girl inside me. But have found that if being popular left someone out, I just wouldn't feel right about that. Even though I know in my Adult life that people get left out a lot of times. I hate to say this, but there are still Cliques, and it is hard to become part of a set group. Even though we are not in High School anymore, there are some that have not grown out of that mindset. For those that have grown up and found those people you didn't like or were jealous of in School were struggling just like you were, wanting to be accepted and liked by their peers. That taking a test was scary. Having crushes on the Popular girl or boy was normal.

The biggest thing is we are still trying to be accepted even being loved by others. The thing is we all have been made Unique and wonderful to be loved by the ones that God wants to walk beside us. Not all are going to see what God sees in us. Why, because they don't need to? Remembering Beauty is in the eyes of the beholder. Diamonds have rough edges and don't shine until the right Diamond cutter comes along to cut away the rough spots and edges.

So therefore, every season in our life, God has a reason for it.

We moved on from High School and am Moving forward. Not every season was or is easy, but if you feel you are a better person now and have been able to help others along the way, then I would have to say IT WAS ALL WORTH IT!

Love, Margene Wiese-Baier

Jeremiah 29:11

Chapter 8

Home Is Where the Heart Is!

They say Love is where the Heart is. I have been on a Journey for a while now. I first went to Florida from Oregon because I wanted to not be tempted to go back into a relationship. Not because I hated that person, but because I know women and how they will go back time and time again into a relationship they should flee from. I did not want to come back to Oregon until I knew I would not be tempted. I have been back a few times now, and left thinking I would not want to move back.

On my Journey, I have been to several locations. I went to Florida for 15 years, Pennsylvania, and Georgia, and now I'm back in Oregon. Loving each place in different ways.

I feel I am being led by the Holy Spirit and being obedient to HIS calling on my life. Remembering what Pastor Freda King told me, "Go where you are Celebrated and not just Tolerated." The thing is that we are put in certain families for a reason. We may not know that reason until God brings us full circle back to where we started. God's timing is everything. There was lot to learn before HE brought me back. The one thing I know is that my Daddy is a very special man and truly hungers and thirsts for the Word of God. He wants to listen to me when I talk about Jesus. He loves his children and wants the best for them. God has placed in him a loving and compassionate heart for others. He has been a caregiver to many. Now it is His children's turn to give back to him.

So home is where my HEART is. For now, that place is back where I began—Oregon, the place I grew up, the place I had my little family, the place I call home. I will go where God leads me. Unfortunately, we don't always appreciate those that we hold dearest in our hearts, until God brings us full circle. Truly healing from our past will make us confront things that we thought we dealt with long ago. We have a loving, compassionate God that will not only heal your heart but heal those that we not only meet along the way but those that we have carried with us.

Please pray for your families. He might bring you back to help you heal but go to HIM and ask what you need to do to Move Forward in your life. Most of all, find JOY in all that you do.

Love is always the Answer, for GOD IS LOVE and LOVE IS GOD!

Learn to Love again. Forgive the ones that hurt you. Remember, hurt people hurt people.

Allow them to move forward. It is time. Release them and you release yourself, allowing the doors to open to your DESTINY.

WHAT BIBLE VERSES DO YOU SEE THAT GOES WITH THIS?

LOVE, Margene/Sunwhisp

Chapter 9

Additional Nuggets

My friend Bill Cameron who is now in Heaven used to say that was just a little Nugget when he would say something that held God's wisdom in it. I look forward to seeing him again in Heaven. It seemed he left this World way to soon, but he left an unforgettable imprint upon many of our hearts.

Childlike Faith

Do you have Childlike faith? I pray that you remember the first day that you fell in love with JESUS. It should be the most Wonderful Memory that you have. I don't remember the exact date, but I do know who first told me about HIM. That was my Mother. My Mom is now in Heaven, since 1985. It is a wonderful Gift that you can give to your Children. You may not be perfect, and you may make a lot of mistakes on the way, but if you can hold onto the LOVE of JESUS, You will be OK, and Well, Give the Gift of JESUS today and remember your Childlike Faith. All is Well in the Name of JESUS. Amen and Amen. Shalom. Margene Wiese-Baier

PS
You can take that into every year. A good thing. Whoop! Whoop! ❤

You Have Blessed Me by Your Love
2017

I am Humbled and so blessed by many of you that have continued to show me Love and respect. God has shown me much about myself. If you ask, HE shows you who you really are. HE has brought many things back to my Memory about my life. The good and the bad. The people that I have loved more than they loved me. The people that didn't love themselves enough to know how much God loved them. HE has shown me the Prophecies that have yet to be fulfilled. HE has brought back the words that HE gave me that no one else had been told. Even the things that HE gave others, but they would not give me because they just could not see me as what God was showing them. I am finding the best Prophecies are from people you don't know. Like Jesus, family, and people in his own hometown did not accept who HE was. I want to encourage everyone that has a word from the Lord. Even though it has not come to pass yet—I say Yet because GOD is a

Promise Keeper—keep believing. It is an exciting day we live in. I believe Abba Father is speaking. Quiet yourself and Listen. HE is waiting to speak to you. Love is the Answer. Speak it loudly. Many need to hear you. Most of all, they need for you to demonstrate it. Hugs.

One Day You Found Me

(Sunday, July 15, 2012)

One day you found me
All Crumpled and Ashamed
Like a Crumpled Piece of Paper in the Rain
My Story was written
And I had nothing to gain
I felt like a sad little Urchin
And I felt a lot of pain

Then You found me
And my life has never been the same
You gave me the Will to live again
My story was re-written
Then I had everything to gain

How can I repay you?
Only You can know
Because You loved me
When I had nothing to Show
You took my crumpled little life
And took out the Strife

You made it plain
That I had everything to gain

Now I walk in Victory
And a Love renewed
I give everything
I have to give to YOU
For I gave myself
That is all that You asked
But YOU gave me more
When You died upon the Cross
My Sins have been forgiven
And all that I know
I will live with YOU forever
The Lover of my Soul

I now have the Victory
And know YOU will never leave me
You carried me when
I did not know what to do

So

I worship You
I Praise Your Name
Cause my life will never be the same
Hallelujah
Hallelujah
Hallelujah
YOU are so Worthy

My Facebook Page

When you come on my page, it is like you are coming into my HOME. I am allowing you to see me as I am in my HOME. This is my SANCTUARY, My MINISTRY ONLINE. I ask that as it is in coming into anyone's home, that you respect them. You do not have to agree with everything I post or even say, but I share my HEART with you to let you know me. I do not stand before you to say that you are supposed to idolize me or to say, "Look at me, I am so wonderful, but I am the KING'S KID, and HE loves me and is watching over me. I pray openly, I Praise and Worship HIM openly." If any one of you don't like that or think I am wrong to do that, then you are not meant to come into my HOME, My page, but if you love the FREEDOM to LOVE HIM the WAY HE Shows you...

I could say more, but I think you get my gist, and my main goal is to show the LOVE of JESUS for others. If you are seeing something else, you are not seeing me.

Margene/Sunwhisp ♥

Father, Today first of all, I THANK YOU that I woke up to seek YOUR WISDOM. YOU have led me into things that I didn't think I knew anything about, but YOU have placed in my mouth, YOUR WORDS, allowing them to flow through my fingers.

Father, YOU have shown me that all I need to do is present them to others, and YOU will be doing the work on their HEARTS and showing me that we are to hate evil, not the people. We are to pray for them that are wondering and seeking for YOU but don't know it. We are not to Condemn but allow YOU to work through us to Convict. Without LOVE, I am but a clanging bell. Father, all I want to do is allow people to see YOUR LOVE through me, In Jesus's Name! Amen and Amen!

Margene ❤

Prayer

I will come boldly before the THRONE and pray. Sometimes, people don't realize prayer is a Conversation with our Father, and they need to know that. God knows my HEART, and HE holds me in the Palm of HIS HAND. It is about Relationship with HIM, not a Religion. HE leads me in the direction that HE has for me. So pretty much I listen to HIS voice only. All others are null and void that would like to convince me that I am to do it their way. I will not be controlled or manipulated by any man or woman.

All this came from a conversation I had with the person who posted these Bible verses, trying to tell me that I should not be praying openly on my page. Sorry, I will not be manipulated or controlled, and if you don't see that God gets all of the Glory on my pages, it is time to move on. I embrace all of you that want to move on to better things with me. It is HIM, JESUS, that is our Anchor and Strength. Without HIM, we are nothing.

Margene/Sunwhisp ♥

What Is Holding You Back

What holds you back the most? Self? Poverty Attitude? The enemy? People? In the wrong place? Job? Well, I think one of the biggest things that hold people back is a Poverty Attitude. I heard a story this morning about a man that was told all his life that he was an idiot, and a teacher even told that person he might as well quit School and get a full-time job. Still believing that he was a nothing, he dressed the part, acted the part until one day at his job, they decided to give him an Aptitude test, and he was found to be a Genius. From that day forward, he started dressing the part and got a better job and became very successful. What changed? The voice that was directing him changed. What does the Father say about you? HE does not condemn us but loves us. HE knew us before the Foundations of the Earth and in our Mother's Womb. So the next time we hear a voice telling us that we are nothing, let that voice know that you are something because you are the KING'S KID. I believe God is up to something, and it is good. What do you have in your HAND? It may just be the KEY to your SUCCESS! And for you single people, you don't have to wait to get

Married before you do something great. You have the most precious PERSON in your LIFE Already. Just a thought...or is it?

We Were Given a Heart

We were given a HEART to know how other people feel. More importantly to know how GOD feels about that person. Before you speak, check your own heart in how you would feel if they said certain things to you. Words can either encourage or destroy. Remembering the enemy is out to Kill, Steal, and Destroy. Words are like a double-edged sword. Like a child, if you only see the mistakes they have made and you only talk to them at that time and forget all the good things they have done, you are more than likely destroying your relationship that you have with them. The same with your other relationships.

If the only thing you received from Abba Father was negative words, you would not continue to talk or listen to HIM. Remember that is not from HIM but from the enemy and his little wannabes. Cherish the Loving Heart HE has given you. When you want to lash back at a person that has hurt you, Allow the Holy Spirit to not only heal your heart, but pray for them that they see you only as GOD sees you. HE has a way of making all things that seem so wrong right again. HE has made you the person you are for a reason.

You are uniquely made. And most of all, HE has qualified you for the Destiny HE is bringing you to. Don't try to be like anyone else. They have to walk their own path to their Destiny, just like you are on your path. Many people may walk beside you for a while, but not all are meant to walk the full distance. The ones that are will not jump ship when you are about to make it but will be there to see you through. Many will help you along the way. Many will be used by the enemy to tell you that you are not what GOD tells you are. The most important things is not to give up. You may think that you are destined for one thing, and GOD may even have a bigger plan for you. We never think as BIG as HE does. When no one else encourages you, encourage yourself like David did.

Love, Margene

1 Samuel 30:6
New International Version

> *David was greatly distressed because the men were talking of stoning him; each one was bitter in spirit because of his sons and daughters. But David found strength in the LORD his God.*

While living in St. Petersburg in my own Apartment, I had many encounters with The

Father. On one particular day, I was deep in Worship and Praise, and I was praying that I would get to know HIM more. I can't say that I had a vision, but I knew HE was there. I heard Him tell me that one of HIS names was Yahweh, and HIS favorite name was Father. I was so over-whelmed with Joy and Happiness in my Spirit. At that point in my life, I did not remember ever hearing anyone ever calling HIM Yahweh, let alone reading it. Of course, soon after that, I heard songs and people calling HIM, Yahweh. I heard people praying to the Father, but that evening was super special to me. I had many other encounters in that Apartment. I even went to Church, and a Prophet told me that I had many very large Angels around me for protection.

I did not go back on the Internet for years because of the devastation caused from my inter-action with Detective Coolhand, but when I did, I started many Ministry Pages on Facebook. All directed by God. HE told me to get Admins for the pages because I would not have time to watch over all of them. He led me to some good and faithful people. One, I even told that he was a Pastor, and he said, "How did you know that?" Well, God told me. He later asked to be released from the Page he helped me with because he got an assignment with a local Church in his area. I had one woman that was telling me that I should not tell people when I was going through a bad time. She said, being a Pastor, I was held to a higher accountability. I finally asked her to leave because she was reprimanding me saying this on my page, and I felt it not only dishonored me but God. (I felt she could have come to me privately and texted me instead of on my public page.) I also had some good and faithful helpers, too many to mention here, but they know who they are, and more importantly, Abba Father knows who they are, and I pray a thousandfold blessing upon them and their family's life.

I still am on Facebook doing my Ministry. I know it has touched many people even if they don't say anything or click on the Like button. I know that the important thing is that I was obedient in making the pages. I just want to follow where HE leads me. In Jesus's Name!

Esther Nights

One night after working at the Furniture store in Englewood, Florida, I went home to my little Bungalow. I put on my favorite dress and turned on some Praise and Worship Music, and I began to dance before my King. I was so entranced in my Worship that at first, I didn't notice that people's names and faces were coming up in my spirit. I loved getting together with friends and doing Worship, but this was the first time I felt like this was an Esther night.

I began praying for the people the Lord presented for me. One man in particular was my coworker at the Furniture Store. He was separated from his wife and said he wanted her back. So I intensely prayed for them to reunite. I knew the Lord was listening to me. I continued until I felt a release to stop praying for people. I then thought that this was something I should start with a group of women from the Church.

The next day, I went to work and told this man that I had prayed for him and his wife. It was amazing what he told me. The same time I was praying, he had met his wife on the beach. The amazing thing was for one, it was the same time I was praying, and this man hardly ever went to the Beach. The next thing he said is he didn't know if he really wanted to get back together with her or not. I told him that he needed to make up his mind because I cannot pray for him to get back together with her and him being double minded. Apparently neither one of them wanted to get back together, and they got a Divorce. I learned that day you cannot pray against a person's Will.

God showed me what that night meant. That Esther was an Intercessor. She interceded for her people, the Jews, to be set free and protected. And therefore, that night I interceded for my friends and family.

I later asked the Pastors at the Church I was going to about having Esther nights and was not granted to have them. But I did go to a party at a house, and one of my friends was there. We talked about Esther Nights, and she had been thinking about them too. She was able to do them at that Church. I planned on just doing them after I was refused but have not done them Yet! Maybe the time just was not right. I no longer live in Florida, so I am just following Abba Father's lead.

I always loved the Father, Son, and Holy Spirit, but I didn't really know that I knew I wanted to be in Ministry. I always tried to be a good person, and I loved Jesus with all my heart. I prayed not only for myself but for others, especially my family, friends, and my pets. Seeing many of my pets healed after praying for them. It brought great joy to my Heart to be used by my Abba Father.

Our Job as Children

Our Parents took care of us from the time we were born till we left their house. So when the time comes, it is our turn to take care of them. The Roles are reversed. That is the way it is supposed to be.

My job as a DAUGHTER is to love my Parents forever. To want to be there for them no matter how close or far away I am. To stand up for them when others try to take advantage of them and that means being bold enough to say, "That is my Mom or Dad, or Parents, and you have no right to treat them that way."

As our parents get old, there are many people out there just waiting like vultures to sweep down on them and Steal, kill, and destroy them.

Unfortunately, some of them are their own family. Sad but true. Waiting in the Wings to take them for everything they have.

We as Children have to make our parents aware that we will be there if they need us. Not waiting for them to die, so we can have whatever they have. But to help them to live safely and comfortably for the rest of their time here.

My dad came home the other day and said, "I am sure glad I have the kids I have." I asked him what he meant, and he said, "Some kids really don't care anything for their parents." I am saddened by that statement. Every day, I miss my Mom, and would want her back, but I know she is in Heaven and won't have to go through what my Dad's friend is going through with Dementia.

I love my Dad with all my Heart. God gave me a treasure when HE gave me such a wonderful Dad. I am here with him to appreciate this time together. To help him. Actually, we help each other by encouragements and being there when needed. Not a sacrifice, but a privilege. Many people have said, "Do you realize how lucky you are to still have your Dad. So enjoy each moment you have with him."

I see it as such a Blessing. I would love that he would live forever, but I know that someday I will have to say goodbye to him. But I will just say at that point, "Bye, I will see you later in Heaven."

As I am writing this, my Dad will be 93 March 12th. Woo-Hoo!

I Believe!

2010

> *For God so loved the World that He sent His only Begotten Son that whosoever believes in Him will not perish but have everlasting Life. For God did not send His Son into the world to condemn the world, but that the world through Him might be saved. (John 3:16–17)*

I am a Supernatural being having a Human experience. To just be a Human would be boring.

I believe there is a God that is here to help us, and I believe there is an enemy that is here to torment us.

I believe there is a Heaven and a Hell. They are both very real.

I believe that God sent His Son, Jesus, to die and be raised from the dead and to go back to Heaven to sit at His right side so I can go to Heaven myself one day.

I believe He knew me before the very foundation of the World and that He mapped out a Plan and a Purpose for my Life. As it is said in Jeremiah 29:11, I do not hold lightly the things the LORD has given me. To HIM, I give all of the Glory! People will come and go in my life, but HE will walk beside me for all Eternity. HE is a JUST GOD and looks into the Heart of every believer. I am excited to see all that HE has revealed to me. As I write, I am seeing New revelations of where I have been and where HE is bringing me to. HE has brought me out to bring me IN. I LOVE HIM more today than yesterday. A BELIEVER in JESUS.

Ask HIM how HE sees you, and I know HE will call you Son or Daughter.

Victory in Jesus.

Love and Abundant Blessings, Margene/ Sunwhisp, 2017

Eagles and Eaglets, It Is Time to Soar

Thank you all for your prayers on this part of my Journey in Oregon. Going where God wants you to go is sometimes very difficult and hard to do, not because it is not a good thing, but you sometimes have to leave people that you love, even if it is just for a little while. I have had to even leave animals behind, and that is difficult enough. I cried on the plane because I missed my two daughters and grands so much and I'd barely lifted off the ground. I have been on a Journey all my life but have been really trying to see what GOD has set before me. I have had some Divine appointments and have even met with some Disappointments. But knowing that whatever comes my way to Seek the Kingdom and HIS guidance, and I will be fine. Thankfully, HE has made me adaptable to all these changes. People have so many different personalities and expectations of me. But I am thankful HE never leaves me or forsakes me. People keep asking me what I am doing, and all I can say is I am going where GOD leads me. Sorry, I can't say exactly what I am doing because HE has not shown me everything yet. It is like HE just gives me a little bit, a step I am to take, because I may not go if I knew everything. Like Jonah. HE said, "Go to Nineveh." HE did not go when HE was first told. I do not want to be like him. I want to hear the directions and go and not have it come around again. Learning to hear HIS Voice is priceless. I treasure this Adventure. Being where HE wants you to be is where you are supposed to be. I know now more than ever when there is a delay, it is a blessing, and there is a reason for it. Healing is enabled, and Divine Love can come—will, to be continued.

I speak LIFE into myself. All exhaustion, Anxiety, and pain must leave my body. I have work to do for the KINGDOM! I do not have time to be in a slumbering state. I LOOK above to Abba Father for all my help. I ask that my Angels are dispatched to go ahead of me in all my Journeys. I am Destined with a Plan that HE alone has ordained. People may not understand these things, but the People that do will be for me and not against me. I will walk on water and Soar like the Eagle. I am Triumphant! I am Above and not beneath. I am whom my Father said I am. I do not have to defend myself to anyone because

HE already is my defense, my Vindicator. I am Victorious in Jesus's Name. Like liquid gold, he slathers me with HIS Love and gentleness. He will whisper to me all the things HE wants for me. HE has placed in me the Heart of Love. HE has placed in me Compassion for others. HE releases in me all that HE has for me in the right time and the right season.

Chapter 10

Moving Forward to a New Chapter in My Life

This may be the end of this book, but it is not all of my story or the end of my Story. There are parts that I either forgotten or didn't see as important to add. I still have some living to do. I have not reached my Destiny yet. Those things are to be Continued in another book.

Most of all, I wanted this book to help people that have gone or are going through things that are similar to what I have gone through.

I believe that is why we go through trials and tribulation—not because God wants to hurt us. Besides, some things I believe the enemy was allowed to do these things with Abba's permission, like Job. But HE never leaves us or forsakes us and always gives us a Door of escape. Like my Dream about a bird in a cage. One day the cage was set outside, and it was knocked over, and the Bird flew away. That was Freedom. I believe that bird was me. I had that dream after I got a Divorce. Many times, even though I felt trapped in a Situation,

HE gave me a way out. I don't know about you, but I love closed doors when I am trying to make a decision. It shows me that I do not have to ponder what I need to do. HE is already showing me the way to go.

I always pray for my Unbelief. And that HE helps me in that area. Having the faith of a Mustard Seed is all I need sometimes. With every answered Prayer, my Faith is built. Every Prayer that seems like a no may not be a denial but "wait for something better." I like the song by Garth Brooks that says, "Thank God for unanswered prayers." I can remember several times I could have said that. There are other times when I wish I would not have had my way but have learned not to force my way instead of God's way. May HIS Will be done, not mine. In Jesus's Name, I pray. So time to move Forward!

*This is from a photo my sister took
of me that I put in Photomania*

Margene Wiese-Baier

Self-portrait pastel

Photos of me Cartooned by PhotoMania App

www.ingramcontent.com/pod-product-compliance
Lightning Source LLC
Chambersburg PA
CBHW051151120626
46547CB00012B/1036